HOW TO GET
YOUR LOVER BACK
WAS WRITTEN FOR YOU IF . . .

- Your lover walked out the door and you want him or her back

- Your lover is physically with you, but not really present

- The breakup occurred long ago but you never really understood why and you want to know now

- You're not really sure you even want your lover back, but you want to understand what happened

There is a cure for heartache. It's getting your lover back. Chances are you've tried and it didn't work. Is there really an approach that will not only reunite you and your loved one but make your relationship happier and healthier than before?

There is. And it's simple and will build your self-esteem in the process. You can love your lover back to you.

HOW TO
GET YOUR
LOVER BACK

Blase Harris, M.D.

A DELL TRADE PAPERBACK

A DELL TRADE PAPERBACK
Published by
Dell Publishing
a division of
Bantam Doubleday Dell Publishing Group, Inc.
1540 Broadway
New York, New York 10036

ISBN: 0-440-50089-3

Printed in the United States of America
Published simultaneously in Canada

October 1989

20   19   18

BVG

To Maria
at the footbridge
in the valley

ACKNOWLEDGMENTS

That they may know how much their encouragement and suggestions have meant to me, I wish to thank the following persons:

Neal Mazer, M.D., Fred James, Ken Schoolland, James and Margaret Setliff, Kikuko Takai, Debbie Saito, Ann Young, Bruce Dias, Joseph Harris, and Teresa Gagne, who read the manuscript or parts of it in its early form.

Maria Ashley, who read the manuscript in many of its forms, commented on it, and listened to me talk of it endlessly.

Dan Shaw, a computer doctor who still does house calls.

Boyd Slomoff, M.D., who offered to read it, and discussed it with me—though I never did get a copy to him.

K. Y. Lum, M.D.—though I never discussed my book with him, he introduced me to Dr. Tennov's term "limerance."

Irv Cohen, M.S.W., who went out of his way to discuss relevant case histories with me.

Sydney Filson, who showed me how to write a chapter outline.

Birgit Kruse, the best salesperson I know, who patiently encouraged me and shared her views on the Porcupine Technique, the Take-Away, positive visualization, and "shoebox notes."

And my very first editor, Jody Rein, whose genuine interest made the process of editing, believe it or not, pleasant.

CONTENTS

PART IV: LOVE IN THE REAL WORLD

INTRODUCTION

At random, you open up a copy of Emily Brontë's *Wuthering Heights*. You come upon Heathcliff, who is approaching Cathy's deathbed. Cathy is dying of a poorly defined illness—you suspect heartache.

Heathcliff says "wildly," "Why did you betray your own heart, Cathy? I have not one word of comfort. You deserve this. You have killed yourself. Yes, you may kiss me, and cry, and wring out my kisses and tears; they'll blight you—they'll damn you. You loved me—then what right had you to leave me? What right—answer me—for the poor fancy you felt for Linton? Because misery, and degradation, and death, and nothing that God or Satan could inflict would have parted us, you, of your own will, did it. I have not broken your heart—you have broken it, and in breaking it, you have broken mine."

Cathy sobs, "I forgive you. Forgive me!"

Five pages later Heathcliff is informed of Cathy's death. He cries out to her ghost, "I know that ghosts have wandered on earth. Be with me always—take any form—drive me mad! only do not leave me in this abyss, where I cannot find you! Oh God! it is unutterable! I cannot live without my life! I cannot live without my soul!"

There is no grief quite like the grief of love lost. Suddenly the world, no matter what the season of the year, becomes a cold, indifferent place. The drizzly gray November of northern latitudes takes possession of your soul. The flavor has gone out of food, the beauty out of nature. Even if your lover has left you at the height of spring, the budding and newly green trees may as well be the dead, leafless sticks of autumn, pointing jagged fingers at steel-gray skies—no matter that the sky is actually blue, full of white clouds, warm breezes, and the scent of flowers. You are but dimly aware of the former pleasures of life. An invisible layer of numbness has enveloped your body. You have lost your interests. Life has lost its meaning.

Getting out of bed has become an incredible burden. How are you going to get through a day's work? Another day in an endless succession of days. This can't be happening! Not to you! Your relationship was different, it can't be over! Other people, though, if they notice at all, will just shake their heads and may think, *Oh, yeah, there goes another one,* and may say, "He'll (she'll) get over it." What else can they say? Despite all the songs and movies, or perhaps because of them, the world is indifferent.

Your friends worry about you. They counsel you, "There's more than one fish in the sea." "Don't be an adolescent about it." "He didn't deserve you anyway." "You've got to go on with your life."

How are you going to tell people that she or he left you? The guilt . . . If only you had done things differently, maybe this wouldn't be happening.

And there is another peculiar thing. All they say about heartache, about the seat of love being located in the heart, it must be true. You know that the brain is where the action is supposed to be, but that strange, empty, lonely longing, as if someone has run off with a piece of your soul, is located just a little left of center within your chest, literally where your heart ought to be.

You experience an incredible need to be reassured by your lover, to be held, to be told that you are still loved, to be allowed to say that you do love . . . the need to discover that the breakup was all a mistake, that your lover is coming back, sooner or later is coming back, that you will have another chance. The emptiness cries out to be filled with your lover's embrace. Your needs wrack you, demand satisfaction *now*, perhaps even lead to anger. Paradoxically, ironically, it is all this neediness, especially neediness out of control, that most threatens your chance of getting your lover back.

In my practice as a psychiatrist when I prescribe a medication, I am sometimes asked if I've tried it myself. The answer is usually no. It is not wise to take medication unless it is necessary, nor is it necessary to experience every possible disruption of intellectual and emotional well-being in order to help those who are experiencing such disruptions. When I'm asked, however, if I've ever taken my own prescription of the advice in *How to Get Your Lover Back*, my response is different.

The approach presented here to getting a lover back is based on my studies during my training as a psychiatrist, on my observations of the lives of others, and on my own experiences. I have seen it work in the lives of others, but the inspiration to write this book occurred after I successfully used this approach in my own life.

I had been in a number of relationships that had gone sour. There is always a sadness when a relationship ends, even when one prefers that it end. Sometimes I fought desperately to save a romance, or thought I did, even though deep down I had to admit my fear was that I might succeed in making the romance last longer. I needn't have feared. I was using all the standard techniques that people use in such situations—insisting, pleading, caving in on issues that were important to me, demanding, getting jealous—all the techniques that are guaranteed to chase a lover away forever.

Then the day came when I *really* didn't want to lose my lover. I should have realized it sooner, but I hadn't, and that's the way things go sometimes. I had neglected a relationship to the point that to any outside observer, as well as to myself, the inside observer, it was too late. I began to respond in my usual way, suddenly promising all kinds of changes, insisting, begging and so on. To make matters worse, by the time I had begun paying attention to what was happening, there was already someone else, and—the worst of all fates for an abandoned ex-lover like myself—the other guy, from what I could tell, was decent, caring, and probably capable of genuinely loving my former, but one and only, true love. Finally my former lover had discovered the kind of attentiveness in a relationship she rightfully expected. And there I was making demands, trying to make her feel guilty, to break her away from what seemed to be making her happy. I was headed for an inevitable loss, and I knew it.

So I decided, *not this time.* If I really loved her, and she had really loved me, if I really understood the human psyche, if my unshrinklike belief in true love wasn't naive, I ought to be able to figure out how to get my lover back— this time it counted. I did, and I got her back.

One case does not prove a point, but the technique involved is not based on a case, it is based on the fundamental premise that the person using it genuinely loves his or her lover. The rest follows logically.

How to Get Your Lover Back is divided into four sections. Part I, "Evaluating Your Situation," helps you to explore where you are, so that you can think about your answers to the very personal questions "Should I get my lover back?" "Am I prepared to devote the time and energy required to developing the skills and psychological strength necessary to sustain a genuine loving bond?" and "What do I mean by love?" Then we look at the more general questions "What is the nature of love?" and "How are lasting loves formed?"

With these questions explored, we can begin part II, "Preparing for Contact" with your ex-lover. This preparation will help guard against the common mistakes that anxious lovers often make before *you* make them; it explores ways of coping with the lonely times when you cannot be with your lover.

Part III, "Getting Back Together," the goal of the book, will help you examine, *before* potentially confusing situations arise, the role of sex in your relationship then, now, and in the future. It looks at "How to Get Back in Touch," and then how to create constructive patterns of interaction so as to reestablish what I call your *love-bond*—a committed, loving, lasting connection between two people.

"Love in the Real World," part IV, takes a clear-eyed look at dealing with a resistant lover, as well as at how to handle it if you find yourself in a relationship with someone who lacks the skills required to sustain a mature romantic love-bond and other possible conundrums in which many a frustrated lover has found herself. And then we look at the ultimate question of how to sustain the romance, the love, and the joy once you get your lover back, in the process exploring the question "In the real world, how long is a love-bond supposed to last?"

In all four parts we will look at basic principles, examine how these principles can be applied, and then make the discussion more concrete by looking at examples. No example is likely to be identical to your situation, but you will probably find many helpful similarities. It is also important to remember that, as in any skill, you only become good at loving if you practice.

If your lover has walked out the door and you want him back, if your lover is physically with you but not really present, if you are not sure you want him back, but you want to understand what happened, or if the breakup occurred a long time ago and you never really understood what happened but you'd like to know, then *How to Get Your Lover Back* was written for you.

PART I

Evaluating Your Situation

"I lay me down upon a bank
Where love lay sleeping
I heard among the rushes dank
Weeping, Weeping"
—William Blake

Chapter 1

OKAY, SO YOU LOST YOUR LOVER

> "To wait an Hour—is long
> If love be just beyond—
> To wait eternity—is short—
> If love reward the end—"
> —Emily Dickinson

Your lover may seem just beyond your grasp, and to pause a moment may seem an eternity; to scream about the grief that has been inflicted upon you may seem the natural thing to do, as if that would shorten the moment, as if that would get your lover back. Relax. The chance of getting your lover back lies in a different direction; it lies in a unique, uncommon response to losing a lover.

Despite your grief, you can learn to love your lover back to you. However, grief and anxiety have a nasty way of impairing the ability to love. So, first, you must take a deep breath and calm down.

If you have been in love with someone, no matter the length of time, watched the bond dissolve away, and now regret the loss, you can once again hold your lover in your arms as fully and closely in love with you as ever. This book will tell you how to do it. It is not a theoretical work, though theory will be alluded to. It is a practical guide.

Too often we treat love as pure magic, undecipherable or decipherable only in some far-removed abstract theory. Love is so wonderful; we are in such awe of it that we feel we show it disrespect, degrade it or ourselves, if we try to analyze and understand it. Yet refusal to understand what we so highly value condemns us to swinging away in the dark like a blindfolded batter hoping to hit the ball, hoping, in fact, that someone has thrown a ball.

If you are willing to step into the light and look at the nuts and bolts of how to get your lover back, you might succeed. Whether or not you are aware of it, there are basic principles of human interaction. If we do certain things in a specified situation, people are likely to respond in a predictable manner. Salespersons, politicians, and advertisers know this. Perhaps it's time that lovers learned as well. Once you learn the principles and get down the techniques that apply those principles, your ex-lover may seem to respond as if he or she were a puppet on strings, but (WARNING!) if you start gloating over your new-found power and jerk the strings just for laughs, you could snap them and lose your lover all over again.

There are definable skills involved in relationships, just as surely as there are skills in tennis, baseball, astrophysics, or driving a car. Most people are so little aware when it comes to what actually goes on in a real love-bond that even a very basic sort of knowledge will put you way ahead. And if, in the area of relationships, you develop a knowledge of basic human nature, your chances of success in getting your lover back are greatly increased.

I have combined insights into the workings of the human heart with, believe it or not, basic sales techniques to develop the approach in this book. The difference between you and a salesperson is that you are not selling some object, for example, a car, that once sold, you can forget about. You are selling yourself as a desirable and loving person. *You cannot afford to sell a lemon.* False advertising will get you nowhere if true love is the goal. You are what you sell. You are telling someone that you love him or her. The surest way to convince is to demonstrate.

If you have been rejected by your lover, you are probably suffering from the pain of a grief reaction. Your pain, need, and anger may block out everything else. Frustrated lovers are often very selfish. They are too caught up in their own anguish to begin to take meaningful steps to get their lovers back. This book is about how to take those meaningful steps. The goal of those steps is retrieval of a genuine love-bond. Nothing short of that will do.

The goal is not merely physical cohabitation with someone you long for. The world is full of people living together who think they are in relationships with lovers but actually in their hearts they know that though they may be in a relationship of sorts, there are no "lovers" involved. A love-relationship based predominantly on guilt, pity, fear, need, habit, or some other love-substitute is worse than no relationship at all.

A true love-bond is a growth experience and, ideally at least, involves healthy people. A love-bond is not something at which one desperately clutches. If your relationship has become a clutching one, then the bond that holds you to your lover will in time have little or nothing to do with love, and, in truth, you will then need to get your lover back as much as the person whose lover has already physically left.

Falling in and out of love is not some kind of magic. It is a natural process that can be understood and mastered. Once you have been in love with someone, it is possible to remain so for a lifetime.

Love properly understood can be love regained. This book will show you how.

Dispel the pronouncements of your friends. Out of a genuine but misguided concern for your welfare, out of a projection of their own disappointments, or perhaps even out of an underlying jealousy, your friends and acquaintances may have assured you that there is more than one fish in the sea, more than one grain of sand on the beach. Those words are true, but empty! You are in love with a particular fish in the sea and a particular grain of sand. You can see the grain of sand in your hand, its own peculiar shape and facets and pattern of reflected light. It glimmers. That is the grain of sand for you.

You are told, "You can't make it happen."

Or, "If it was meant to be, it would be."

Such statements are as absurd as, "If you were meant to be a piano player, you would be able to play Bach as soon as you sat down to a piano."

Even your psychotherapist, if you have one, may be counseling you that the success or failure of this particular relationship is not the main concern. It may not be his concern, but it is yours. You lie awake nights thinking of this one particular relationship. When you fall asleep, you are plagued by dreams and nightmares. There are moments, especially when you wake in the morning to the fully conscious awareness of your loss, that your soul seems to have been sucked out of your chest and the color out of the world. You want to get your lover back.

This is not necessarily an unhealthy wish. There is something therapeutic to be said for getting a lover back. In fact, there are very good reasons for attempting to get a lover back. You owe it to yourself to consider them. We can begin our discussion of these reasons by looking at what it is that brings lovers together in the first place.

There is an old myth that there once was a time when

each of us was whole, but we were cut in half, and each half spends its life looking for the other half. In our lovers we do, in a way, find our missing selves. The missing self could be a character trait, an attitude, or even a physical characteristic. It could be a spontaneity, an artistic sense, an enhanced ability to "feel" or intuit, or an ability to think analytically.

So, is it true after all that opposites attract? Lovers *are* looking for their opposites, but in a special sense of the term. The "oppositeness" need not have anything to do with hair color, and so on. Lovers may very well look alike and be alike in many ways, but there is some essential way in which they are not alike. Your missing part found in another is what gives your love-bond "electricity." Instead of envy for what we lack, envy is turned on its head and becomes love. (For a detailed description of the psychology of love as transformed envy, see psychoanalyst Theodor Reik's *Of Love and Lust*.) A burst of joy comes from the discovery of our other self, and we fall in love.

Our lovers don't actually supply the missing half—at least not in a healthy relationship. They provide an opportunity for development of that part in ourselves or, if development is impossible, then a coming to terms with our lack. But the learning process is hard. In a relationship gone bad, love can revert to envy. We deliberately overvalue the part we already are and demean what we are not. Successful lovers use their knowledge of each other to create happiness. Unsuccessful lovers use the same knowledge to inflict pain.

For example, if your lover is too controlled, you may need to learn a little of this control yourself, and, in turn, your lover may need to become more spontaneous. If things don't work out, you become even less controlled. You find it difficult to discipline yourself to a schedule in order to achieve set goals. You lash out at your lover for his lack of spontaneity, making him more uptight about a spontaneous expression of feeling. When we are threatened, we retreat to the familiar. So your nonspontaneous lover becomes less spontaneous. This, of course, is just one, admittedly simplistic, example of how lovers can complement one another and accelerate growth or, if things go wrong, inhibit one another and impede growth.

A lost relationship may be a lost opportunity for growth. A relationship regained can be a regained opportunity for accelerated growth for you and for your lover.

There is another very practical, crucially important reason for getting a lover back. If you don't learn now to make a relationship work, then when? Finding another fish in the sea is not good enough. Sooner or later, in order for any love-bond to work, it is necessary to make a particular love-bond work. It is relatively easy to go from one failed relationship to the next, each time thinking that the previous relationship just wasn't meant to be—some people call this serial monogamy. This seemingly easier course ultimately leads to no love-bond, *ever*, only a series of emotional highs that inevitably slide downhill to another broken relationship. After many a hopeful start, a would-be lover may finally tire of the effort and settle for a dependency-bond that serves to fend off loneliness.

Serial monogamy is the logical consequence of the "more than one fish in the sea" philosophy. The more difficult, but ultimately more rewarding course of action would be to examine *why* a relationship hasn't worked and fix it. If not now, then when? After the next breakup?

We are bound in many subtle and not-so-subtle ways by our own hang-ups and by our inexperience with genuine love, and this prevents us from learning. Any relationship that has been based on love is not only worth saving, it is necessary to try to save it if we are to understand what it is about ourselves that prevents our love lives from working.

Simply to dismiss the issue and blame our failures on our former lovers (or fate) destroys our own chance of growing. Sure, our lovers make mistakes, but learning how to deal with those mistakes is part of love, and in the process we may teach our lovers how to deal with our mistakes. It is possible to learn in the next relationship what we should have learned in the last, but if romantic love is the goal, sooner or later we are going to have to learn how to love romantically. A broken love-bond is a lost opportunity.

But before you learn *how* to get your lover back, you need to ask yourself questions that will help you separate unhealthy from healthy reasons for wanting a lover back. Unhealthy reasons usually arise from a confusion of love with intense emotions that of themselves have nothing to do with love, that may in fact be incompatible with love. For example, salvaging a wounded ego is not a good reason for getting a lover back, although it may "feel" as if it were a perfectly good reason. You may even find yourself rationalizing that this feeling is proof of your love. Intense feelings have a way of blinding us to our own reasons for doing things. We must gain a clear view of our motives and then decide whether they justify getting a lover back.

In my practice as a psychiatrist, I don't tell people what they should do; instead, I ask them questions of a special kind. I try to lead the person in therapy around blind spots so that patterns of behavior and the underlying reasons for that behavior can be recognized. The result is an increased self-awareness that makes possible an informed decision about what to do next. In the same way I would like to ask you a series of questions to help you see beyond the powerful emotions you may be experiencing, so that you may gain a clear view of your motives and can then make an informed answer to the question "Should I get my lover back?"

So it is time to pause and reflect. What follows is a series of twenty-one questions for you to answer. They are designed to help you decide what it is you want to do next. There are no "correct" answers. In this matter there are only your answers. You may find it helpful to use the analysis that follows the questions. The main purpose, however, is to stimulate constructive thought about a very important decision you have to make.

SHOULD YOU GET YOUR LOVER BACK?
(Twenty-one Questions to Think About Before You Decide What to Do Next)

1. I may be hurt and lonely since my lover left me but, still, I have to admit that basically I dislike the kind of person that my ex-lover is.

___ Agree ___ Disagree ___ Not sure

2. I really want a monogamous, romantic relationship.

___ Agree ___ Disagree ___ Not sure

3. If I don't get my lover back, I will kill myself.

___ Agree ___ Disagree ___ Not sure

4. I do my thing; he (she) does his (her) thing; and if that brings us together, it's wonderful.

___ Agree ___ Disagree ___ Not sure

5. It's okay for me to lie to my lover if I do so to avoid hurting him (her).

___ Agree ___ Disagree ___ Not sure

6. It's okay for my lover to lie to me if he (she) does so to avoid hurting me.

___ Agree ___ Disagree ___ Not sure

7. I am willing to change myself in any manner that is necessary to get my lover back.

___ Agree ___ Disagree ___ Not sure

8. If my lover spends time on interests other than me, he (she) should at least keep me informed of *all* those interests.

___ Agree ___ Disagree ___ Not sure

9. Sometimes I think, "If only I had dumped my lover first!"

___ Agree ___ Disagree ___ Not sure

10. I agree with Janis Joplin, "Freedom's just another word for nothing left to lose."

___ Agree ___ Disagree ___ Not sure

11. I am willing to forget my feelings so that I can love my lover 100 percent.

___ Agree ___ Disagree ___ Not sure

12. If I didn't need my lover, I wouldn't try to get him (her) back. ("Need" in the sense of something essential to life, such as air, food, or water, for example.)

___ Agree ___ Disagree ___ Not sure

13. My lover and I used to have fun when we talked together.

___ Agree ___ Disagree ___ Not sure

14. I should be punished for destroying such a beautiful relationship.

___ Agree ___ Disagree ___ Not sure

15. My ex-lover and I talked openly and freely about sex.

___ Agree ___ Disagree ___ Not sure

16. If I could hurt my ex-lover's new lover, I would.

___ Agree ___ Disagree ___ Not sure

17. I should be the center of my lover's life.

___ Agree ___ Disagree ___ Not sure

18. If I don't get my lover back, I'll never fall in love again.

___ Agree ___ Disagree ___ Not sure

19. My ex-lover used to beat me. (In this question "not sure" means, "Well, he kind of just pushed me around." Or, "Yes, but I started it."

___ Agree ___ Disagree ___ Not sure

20. If I could punish my lover, I would.

___ Agree ___ Disagree ___ Not sure

21. I will never know everything there is to know about my lover.

___ Agree ___ Disagree ___ Not sure

THE ANSWERS

1. Agree = −1, disagree = +1, not sure = 0.
Without liking there is no "bond" in a love-bond. Beware of the rationalization that when your lover comes back to you, his basic personality will change. Characteristics and traits may slowly change over time, emotional and intellectual potential may become actualized, but a person's basic personality very rarely, if ever, changes. If you don't like the basic personality of your lover, who are you in love with? A big part, if not the whole part, of "the who" is the personality. If your answer was "maybe," then give yourself time to sort out your feelings. If you need to spend time with your ex-lover to do this, there is nothing wrong with that, but if you are going to go to the trouble of getting your lover back, make sure you like your lover.

2. Agree = +1, disagree = −1, not sure = 0.
Getting a lover back is not only a matter of bonding to a particular person, it is a lifestyle choice. In fact, the clear-

est reason for not getting a lover back is a preference for the single life.

3. Agree = − 1, disagree = + 1, not sure = 0.

To reach the point of suicide as an alternative to getting a lover back is to reach the extreme of pathological dependency, and even if a lover does come back, no love is possible. To say, "I *feel* like killing myself," is different from, "I *will* kill myself," and indicates less dependency and could be a metaphoric description of the grief one experiences at losing something valued.

A yes answer ("I *will* kill myself") is so negative that I considered weighing it down with additional negative points, but the person who answers yes here will gather enough negative points elsewhere to suggest, at the very least, a rethinking of priorities before any decision is made to get a lover back.

4. Agree = − 1, disagree = + 1, not sure = 0.

A yes to this question indicates a willingness to fall in love but not to be in love. If love has any substance at all, it means a commitment to someone else, and commitment goes beyond mere happenstance. It includes a willingness to work at building a love-bond.

5. Agree = − 1, disagree = + 1, not sure = 0.

The truth may be enjoyed or changed or come to terms with, and if you love someone, you may help her to do any one of these three things, but it is hardly loving someone to throw a veil of delusion over reality, even at his own request.

To lie because of fear of violence is justified, but the need to do so indicates a seriously flawed relationship that probably has little to do with a love-bond.

There are situations in which the truth may be implicitly known without being explicitly talked about. For example, suppose you had an affair with someone else last summer and you know your lover knows it, or suspects it, but both of you diplomatically avoid talking about it. However, even here the ability openly to discuss the issue would be the mark of a truly strong love-bond.

6. Agree = −1, disagree = +1 or 0 (see explanation), not sure = 0.

The more someone loves you, the less likely he is to assist you in avoiding reality, even if reality hurts.

If you answered "disagree" to this question, but "agree" to question 5, then shame on you for applying one standard to yourself and another to your lover—you should score this question 0.

7. Agree = −1, disagree = +1, not sure = 0.

A willingness to change oneself "in any manner" indicates a profound disrespect for oneself and is the psychological equivalent of suicide.

8. Agree = −1, disagree = +1, not sure = 0.

The need to be kept informed may be an indication of an unhealthy dependency and/or lack of trust. In a loving relationship, information is spontaneously shared, and there need not be an accounting of *all* interests.

9. Agree = −1, disagree = +1, not sure = 0.

Agreeing to this remark suggests a desire to soothe a wounded ego or even a desire for revenge, neither of which are compatible with a genuine desire to get a lover back.

10. Agree = −1, disagree = +1, not sure = 0.

Janis Joplin's song written by Kris Kristofferson refers to the "freedom" that results from the breakup of a relationship. One is then free to do something else— pursue another relationship, try the single's life, or try to get a lover back. To say that there is "nothing left to lose" goes beyond the natural grief that often comes with a breakup and indicates excessive dependency and a low sense of self-worth.

11. Agree = −1, disagree = +1, not sure = 0.

If a love-bond is to be strong and stable, it is necessary to give priority to love rather than "feelings"; however, it would be very unhealthy to forget your feelings (e.g., anger, sadness, desire). To attempt to do so leads to frustration and resentment. The subconscious does not forget feelings.

12. Agree = −1, disagree = +1, not sure = 0.

If without need, there is no desire to get a lover back, then need (dependency), not love, is all there is.

13. Agree = +1, disagree = −1, not sure = 0.

A lot has been written in romantic fiction, and elsewhere, about intense passionate moments, but what consolidates a love-bond are pleasant times shared together, the more the better. An essential ingredient of pleasant times is the ability simply to enjoy one another's conversation. Without that, no amount of passion can sustain a relationship.

14. Agree = −1, disagree = +1, not sure = 0.

The belief that one needs to be punished is very destructive. Such a belief becomes like a prime directive within the subconscious, so that even without being fully aware, one acts to fulfill the directive. Getting a lover back then becomes more than one deserves, and therefore unlikely. Even if you have destroyed a beautiful relationship, the guilt you may feel should serve as an alarm, not a call for punishment. There is nothing to be gained by beating up on yourself.

15. Agree = +1 or +2 (see explanation), disagree = −1, not sure = 0.

More important than whether or not you believe you and your lover have a good sex life is open and free communication on the subject of sex. Most American couples still have difficulty talking about sex, even in the privacy of their own bedrooms. No matter how good the sex may be—and without plenty of communication it may not be as good as you think—it can be greatly improved by talking about it. Good sex is good communication made physical.

If, in addition to good communication, you and your ex-lover were comfortable with one another when naked in a lighted room, then score this question +2.

16. Agree = −1, disagree = +1, not sure = 0.

The desire to hurt an ex-lover's new lover reflects a lack of self-confidence and, in fact, indicates that one believes the competition is the better lover. Part of loving is accepting the fundamental principle that the person you love has the right to choose who he or she will love. There is no point in blaming "the competition."

17. Agree = −1, disagree = +1, not sure = 0.

Your lover should be the center of her own life, and the more that she is, the more effective is her capacity to love others, including you. Another way of saying this is that a person must love himself before he can love others. If you are in a romantic love-bond with someone, then you are a very important part of that someone's life, but, in a healthy relationship, you are neither the only part nor the center. To demand that you be so is to insist on psychological dependency, which is hardly a loving thing for you to do.

18. Agree = −1, disagree = +1, not sure = 0.

Most people who experience a permanent breakup end up in another relationship. That is because individuals tend to have orientations to particular lifestyles. A person is unlikely to enjoy a happy life in any love-bond if the couple's life is not already his or her preferred lifestyle.

Sometimes the reason a love relationship doesn't work out is that a person with an orientation to a single's lifestyle is trying to force himself into that of the couple. Some people are happier as singles but get caught up in the passion of the moment and try to force a love to work.

When their love inevitably fails, naturally they say, and really mean, that they will never fall in love again.

19. Agree = −2, disagree = +1, not sure = −1.

If "used to beat" means you were beaten until your lover left you, then you can expect more beatings when you get your lover back, unless you are very careful to set limits—including taking legal action if necessary. Even then, it's difficult enough to make a relationship work without getting involved with someone who has demonstrated a profound impairment in his ability to love. Such an impairment does not go away simply because there has been an apology or pleasant intervening moments. You must be very careful to make sure that in some way you are not deliberately seeking out problem relationships; bear in mind that most people claim they aren't deliberately looking for problems even if every romance they've ever been in has involved an impaired lover.

If beatings occurred, but really do belong to the past, you must be careful to make sure that some other form of abuse has not taken their place. Remember, you are loving no one, neither yourself nor your lover, by tolerating abuse.

Being pushed around may not be as bad as getting punched, but it is a gross form of disrespect and, if tolerated, could be a prelude to more severe forms of disrespect.

"Yes, but I started it" may mean that both you and your partner have given priority to anger over love, but it is also a phrase used by those who do not want to admit that their lover is not loving them.

20. Agree = −1, disagree = +1, not sure = 0.

Anger is a natural enough response to being rejected by a lover, but giving priority to anger, which is what one does by wishing to punish a lover, will make for a very unhealthy and unstable love-bond.

21. Agree = +1, disagree = −1, not sure = 0.

People who love and are loved continue to discover hidden potentials in themselves and in those whom they love. The belief that you know everything there is to know about your lover closes down the possibility of the ongoing mutual discovery process that is an essential quality of successful loving.

EVALUATING THE RESULTS

This test is meant to be a general guide to help you determine whether or not you should attempt to get your lover back. The closer to +22, the more you ought to consider, and the more you are likely to succeed at, getting your lover back. If your score is closer to −22, then not only is there less chance of success but if, against the odds, you do get your lover back, even success is not likely to be a happy event. Scores hovering closer to 0 may indicate confused feelings and/or beliefs, not an uncommon state of affairs in someone who has been rejected by a lover. Think about the questions, read the book, come back and think about your responses again. Perhaps your answers will change. That's okay. This is an "open book" test. Whatever your score, *you* must decide what you do next.

Chapter 2

LOVING 100 PERCENT TO GET YOUR LOVER BACK

Loving 100 percent is the key strategy of this book. All other strategies are built upon it. It is therefore essential to understand clearly what is meant by *loving 100 percent*.

LOVING 100 PERCENT

I often hear the complaint "I've done my share. I've given 50 percent. If he would only do his part."

Fifty percent is not enough. Relationships, even under the best of circumstances, require giving 100 percent. This is the most basic principle. Another way of saying this is, you must love your partner 100 percent. Forget the tally sheet. If you genuinely give, you will receive a return. If you are more interested in nit-picking and feuding, carefully checking the tally sheets and demanding that justice be done, you belong in a courtroom, not a relationship. With a good lawyer in the courtroom maybe you can get more than 50 percent. If you are married and keeping score, the courtroom is where your relationship may end up, unless of course religious conviction or social censure dooms you to a lifetime of incessant bickering and/or the cold war of "the silent treatment."

Loving 100 percent does not mean that you should tolerate an assault on your physical, emotional, or financial well-being—that's abuse. You should not allow your lover to grind his heel on your foot while you declare your love, nor should you allow yourself to sink into financial and emotional ruin in an attempt to support alcoholism, compulsive gambling, compulsive buying, and so on. To tolerate abuse not only is not love, it is a renunciation of love, both of oneself and of one's lover. If you persist in tolerating abuse, you may still get your ex-lover physically back with you, but the abuse will return with your ex-lover, and any remnant of real love will steadily diminish. Tolerated bad habits do not make bad habits go away.

THE NEED TO SEPARATE LOVE FROM ADDICTION

Is loving 100 percent loving someone too much? Is it really possible to love your lover too much?

To answer these questions requires us to separate "love" from "addiction." It is common for one human being to become addicted to another and call the addiction *love*. An addiction to a relationship is an attitude, in many cases an acknowledged belief, that the beloved is necessary for life itself. This mind-set has a limiting effect on what one is capable of doing with life. There are no longer any choices. The lover either possesses his beloved or there can be no happiness and life can have no meaning. The ever-present threat of the loss of happiness, or of life itself, effectively destroys genuine love, because the addict's primary concern is to make sure that the loved one is held on to at all costs. The shaky ground she stands on—her profound dependency on someone else—affects her every move.

Contrast this with the lover who has learned first to love himself. Though he may experience unpleasant moments, his basic happiness and underlying confidence remain intact.

The biochemical foundation of romantic relationships is just beginning to be understood. Though the "chemistry" that bonds couples together may find its most profound expression in shared sexual orgasm, the chemistry between lovers affects everything they do. Lovers associate the image, sound, touch, and smell of each other with the pleasant chemistry they experience when they are together, and as a result the bond between them grows stronger. A friend of mine once described to me the emotional impact of spotting her lover's toe in a crowd across a room. Anyone who has ever fallen in love can testify to that kind of impact.

The biochemical foundation that bonds two human beings together can be the first step toward a genuine love-bond, the kind of bond that is based on caring instead of need. However, in a person who has never learned to love himself, it is likely to be the first step to a relationship addiction. In relationship addiction a lover becomes dependent on someone else for his sense of self-worth. This someone else becomes the only road to salvation. In the case of a breakup, the heartbreak of withdrawal is overwhelming. Most important, in a relationship addiction, need becomes more important than love.

Addiction parading as "love" is what Robin Norwood is talking about in *Women Who Love Too Much,* and Stanton Peele in *Love and Addiction.* In truth, the "loving too much" has more to do with a lack of love than with too much of it. It is possible to choose relationship addiction as a substitute for self-love, but to confuse the longing need of relationship addiction with love of self or of another is a profound mistake. Men and women who claim to "love too much" merely substitute a euphemism for the manipulation they engage in to get their needs met. It is unfortunate that they are often manipulated in turn by the people who are the objects of their desire.

Well-meaning observers of addictive "love" usually recommend that the addict find another lover. This recommendation seems to make sense because the love-addict is out of control. However, until relationship addiction is replaced by loving 100 percent, changing partners will merely result in replacing an old addiction with a new one. Loving 100 percent requires the love-addict to change her relationship style, not necessarily the object of her love.

THE PROPER ROLE OF GRIEF AND GUILT

When a lover walks out on you, you may ask yourself, "What did I do wrong?"

That's a good question. You probably did do something wrong. Your lover may have erred, too, but your own behavior is the most immediately correctable. So why not correct it? At the same time, it is important to remember that to wallow in grief and guilt is to add new mistakes to one already made.

Grief is a healthy human response to a loss. It is a part of a process by which we come to terms with loss. It is an emotional adjustment, necessary to accommodate ourselves to a new life situation but not to be indulged in excessively or prematurely. So long as you and your ex-lover are alive, your relationship is not dead. Relationships rarely ever really die, with the kind of finality that physical death has, so long as both partners are still alive. The important thing to remember is that excessive grief is its own occasion for grief; it binds up time and energy, cripples you emotionally, and makes it less likely that you will get your lover back. As with sleep, you may experience the need to spend some time with grief, but do not overindulge in it any more than you would normally sleep sixteen or twenty-four hours a day. Husband your grief (no pun intended) for the actual death of a loved one or the loss of a fortune, for example, but do not squander it on the breakup of a relationship. To do so is self-defeating.

Like grief, guilt has a very useful function. It is analogous to a smoke alarm that alerts you to a fire. Guilt—when functioning properly—alerts you to the fact that you have betrayed your own principles.

Once a smoke alarm has alerted you to a fire, the whining serves only to distract you and make you less effective. Once guilt has alerted you to a betrayal of your principles, it is time to change your behavior or to change your principles. To wallow in guilt is like staring at the smoke alarm while the house burns down; you are wasting precious time.

The primitive "emotion center" of the brain—the limbic system—does not always respond as quickly as we would like. Guilt does not instantaneously dissipate simply because we understand that it has already served its purpose. Thinking awareness, in the cerebral cortex (the thought center), will help throw the "off" switch on guilt.

Having guilt does not mean that you need to be punished. Even if you have made mistakes, that does not mean that you should submit to abuse.

Here is a pathetic sight: an adult human being reciting a litany of how an ex-lover has taken the car, the bank account, and is threatening legal action to get the house, then saying softly that he does not wish to object because "I love her."

"You mean you're going to let her strip you clean?"

"But I love her."

"Letting her strip you clean is not what I meant by loving her one hundred percent."

"But she wants the house."

"And you must not want her for a lover. One day when you wake up to what is happening, you are going to be very angry at her and at yourself."

"I could never be angry at her. If only she would love me like she used to, I would do anything for her."

"Not true. You're too busy beating yourself up to know what you want or to begin to do what you need to do to get it."

"What do you mean?"

"You're letting her put you in the poorhouse. Next thing you know, you won't be able to afford your therapy sessions with me."

"Don't you care? All you're interested in is money."

"I care, but you're going to have to care too. Doesn't it seem that your remark about money applies more to your wife than it does to me?"

THE IMPORTANCE OF MAINTAINING SELF-RESPECT

One of the peculiar traits of human nature is that when one human being sees another degrading herself, as often as not the observer can't seem to resist the impulse to join in the process of degrading the victim by using aggressive words or actions or, somewhat less overtly, by feeling pity for the victim. There may be some primitive, evolutionary reason for this, but unless this trait is kept in mind, you may turn your loving friend into a sadist and yourself into a masochist as you beat yourself silly with guilt, rendering the retrieval of the love of your life less likely with every blow.

Even barnyard chickens, who normally treat one another with a certain modicum of respect, when they see one of their peers tolerating abuse, join in until the poor victim is pecked to the ground and literally walked all over.

This brings us to a significant corollary to the principle of maintaining self-respect: It is almost never wise to cry in front of your lover if the crying is because he has left you. It is all right to cry over the suffering of a child, the death of a dog, a well-acted play, or even a beautiful work of art, but it is *almost* never wise to use tears to twist your ex-lover's arm in an attempt to force a reunion. Your ex-lover may be angry at you, in which case your suffering may be seen as your just reward. On the other hand, your ex-lover may actually comfort you. Your tears may wring pity from his soul, but no matter how pleasant it is to have those arms encircle you again, it is no occasion for joy. You are eliciting sympathetic pity, most likely laced with a little guilt. You are not reigniting the fire of love, in fact, your state will ultimately drive any residual love away. Physical closeness in this instance is deceptive.

Now, I said tears *almost* never work. If your hold on your ex-lover has been exceptionally strong, and if he has not walked too far out the door, then you may snap him right back to you by an open expression of grief, tears, falling to pieces, and so on. If this tactic is not immediately successful, you may be increasing the damage done to an already wounded love-bond, and it would be better to control the tears and any facial expression of grief. Save it for the shoulder of an understanding, *trustworthy* friend or the pillow or a lonely shower, or even explain the situation to a pet dog or the fish in an aquarium; ventilate the emotion, but do not display your grief to your ex-lover.

Pity is not going to revive a love-bond, just as pity does not cause people to fall in love or to be in love. Before attempting to revive a love-bond, it is important to understand what causes us to fall in love and how being in love can develop from such a "fall."

FALLING IN LOVE—NATURE'S FREE GIFT?

Falling in love is nature's free gift. Like the physical act of falling, no exertion is required. There is both more and less to this metaphor than meets the mind's eye.

A fall can be an exhilarating experience, especially if you are unaware of what the conclusion is likely to be. Even if you come prepared with a parachute, impact is a jolt in the best of falls. Most of us have fallen one time or another, usually quite by accident, though there are those hardy parachutists who deliberately jump. But, jump or not, a fall is a fall nonetheless. The likelihood of a fall is increased with certain kinds of activity: Besides the single's scene there's always regular visits to the beach (you could trip over someone) or the art museum, even staying alert at work. But the usual thing about falls is their unpredictability. We fall into situations we wouldn't have expected and, at times, for people we would never have guessed would have tripped us up. Sometimes it's not safe to answer the front door.

Those who have been bruised a few times may become cynics and mock the others who, time after time, pick themselves up, climb back up the great height, and leap again, each time convinced that one of these times they are going to experience the one great exhilarating leap of their life, the one that never ends. Both the cynics, who have given up, and the Pollyannas, who keep jumping, are wrong. Love need not start with a fall, and whether or not it does, it need not end with impact, and this is where the metaphor of "falling in love" is less than it seems.

It is useful to think of falling in love as a kind of psychological "imprinting" of one person on another. The person being "imprinted" is passively falling in love; the image, voice, and so forth of another are, metaphorically speaking, being imprinted on her heart.

In the right setting and at the right time a human being can fall in love with a variety of potential lovers. There are three components to the process of falling in love: *setting, timing,* and *personality match.* Weakness in one or more of these components can be compensated for by strength in another.

A teacher, because of his position of authority in front of the class, may elicit a falling-in-love response from many of his students, even though outside of the classroom he may not fare so well. It is just that within the classroom, the setting and timing are strongly in his favor—*so strongly,* in fact, that many would frown upon his taking advantage of it. This is just one example. A psychiatrist is in an even more powerful position in regard to certain kinds of vulnerable patients, but he would be foolish to assume that his power to elicit the falling-in-love response would persist outside of the doctor-patient relationship. Celebrities and even policemen, when in uniform, are in similar positions. If the personality match, the chemistry, is just right, the timing and setting may not matter as much. And of course, all three—timing, setting, and personality match—can line up at once, a rarer event, but like the lining up of the planets, a celestial experience.

The importance of setting is why lovers go for walks in the moonlight, drink sparkling wine from crystal glasses, snuggle up in a blanket in front of a fireplace on a cold, dark night, and so on. Consciously or unconsciously they are deliberately inducing a love-bond-enhancing, trance-like state.

Just how strong any particular love-bond-enhancing, trance-inducing feature of the environment is depends on the person involved, that person's prior experiences, and probably his or her genetic makeup. That is why people say things such as "The chemistry was just right" when referring to romance. People tend to be attracted to particular types of individuals when it comes to love-bond formations. "Types" may include physical features, personality features, and more subtle traits. Let me give you an example. Let us say a woman has a delightful positive memory of sitting in her father's lap as he smoked his pipe and watched the football game on TV. A woman with a memory of such an experience, especially if the experience occurred more than once and if she has reflected on it over the years, will react differently to a pipe-smoking man who watches football games than a woman who remembers a drunken father who lit up his pipe and slipped into a semistuperous state in front of televised football games.

No matter how intense the falling-in-love experience elicited by setting, timing, and personality match, genuine commitment is not guaranteed, and duration is not necessarily much longer than the time required to get pregnant and "build a nest." To quote John Keats's "Ode to a Nightingale,"

> . . . the fancy cannot cheat so well
> As she is famed to do, deceiving elf.
> Adieu! adieu! thy plaintive anthem fades . . .
> Was it a vision, or a waking dream?

Yet every time we partake of this "vision," we insist that this time it is real. This, we insist, is not like the infatuation we experienced the last time. Of course, while "the last time" was happening, we were convinced that it, too, was "the real thing." Every time we fall in love, we hit the ground, or so it seems. It is my contention that all falling in love is infatuation, but that doesn't necessarily mean that falling in love is a bad thing.

Broadly speaking, falling in love has one of four possible outcomes:

1. The person falling in love may be totally ignored. The emotion of the experience, though it may be intense, will be brief and surely die, usually within a matter of weeks.

2. The person falling in love may be both noticed and ignored. The yo-yo effect of hope alternating with despair can keep the emotion going for years. Related to this is the situation where love is mutual but frustrated by external forces, disapproving families, divergent cultural backgrounds, illness, and so on. Again hope alternates with despair, increasing the intensity (as in William Shakespeare's play *Romeo and Juliet*) and the duration of the experience (as in Emily Brontë's *Wuthering Heights*). The suicides of Romeo and Juliet put a premature end to their falling-in-love experience, just as mutual falling in love without impediment would have.

3. Mutual falling in love without impediment does not last. The glamour and excitement of the new experience wears off. The free ride ends, and in truth it was not a free ride. Nature does not give away energy. The biologically-psychologically induced obsession with the beloved, called "limerance" by the psychologist Dorothy Tennov in her book *Love and Limerance,* repeats itself generation after generation, guaranteeing that no matter what the obstacles, the human species continues to reproduce itself. Limerance makes the beloved seem to glow. It is the trance-state at the heart of the falling-in-love response, but, as we shall see, it is not the same as being in love.

If one partner falls out of love sooner than the other, the other may experience a blow to the ego and a reawakening of the falling-in-love response. That person then attempts to save the relationship, and if successful, this kind of mutual falling in love and out of love, then back in love, can keep going indefinitely (see for example Daisy and Tom Buchanan in F. Scott Fitzgerald's *The Great Gatsby*). A *yo-yo relationship* can go on until death cuts the string.

4. The falling-in-love process is mutual, and one or the other or both lovers begins to truly love. Though the superficial glamour of falling in love fades, it is replaced by something deeper. The free ride, however, is over. If you want a romance that grows deeper *and* continues to glow with excitement, you must work for it. We are talking real love here, not infatuation. It can be a heady experience, but also a little frightening because you are charting the unknown sea within another human being and in the process extending your own capacity to love—the fun of it is that there is no limit. There's a peculiar kind of giddiness, a sensation of sailing through infinite space without end, no impact involved. You have gone beyond the realm of most popular songs.

If a lover assumes that he knows all there is to know about his beloved, then he is no longer a lover. There is far more to a man or woman than whether or not he likes anchovies on his pizza. The potential is infinite. Yet when nature's free ride is over, all too often disappointed lovers assume that's all there is. To make such an assumption creates a self-fulfilling prophecy that comes true with a vengeance. When someone truly loves us, we grow more rapidly than usual, just as added nutrients can speed up plant growth. If someone who used to love us begins to assume that that's all there is, then only our love for ourselves will keep us growing.

WHAT IS LOVE?

Love should not be confused with the need to be loved. We must already be loved—by ourselves—before we are able to love. Love is more than a warm feeling in the center of the chest. In a romantic relationship it is a desire and a commitment to know another human being, to make use of that knowledge in quality time shared with that human being, to be caring for the sake of the joy we experience when we are caring, not for the sake of manipulating someone else into caring for us. At the same time to love is also to set limits, so that we do not allow ourselves to be physically, emotionally, or financially abused.

In *The Art of Loving,* psychologist Erich Fromm defines *love* as "the active concern for the life and growth of that which we love." If there is no faith in continued growth, then love has died. It is amazing that the same man or woman who once said, "I will love you until the end of time," can, once the glow of falling in love has passed, say, "You always were an asshole," or "Don't bother [whatever it is the beloved is bothering to do—quit drugs or write a poem], you'll never be able to do it." Or worse yet, nothing is said. Worse still, there is only the silence of cliché remarks between people who have grown used to the habit of living with one another.

When you buy a record of a popular song, no matter how much you like it, if you play it over and over again, you will tire of it. If you put it away for a while, then bring it back out, you may continue to enjoy it, though perhaps not with the same intensity.

Imagine a magical record that changed a little each time you played it, sometimes going back to the original but varying endlessly in pleasant ways. You would never tire of it. That is what love can do to a relationship.

In attempting to get your lover back, you are trying to start the process over again. You once loved one another, therefore the chemistry is there. You can work on the setting and the timing to cause your ex-lover to fall in love with you again and then continue the process to re-establish the love-bond. It is not even necessary that falling in love occur. You can work on the setting and timing to demonstrate your love, and that is likely to be more than enough.

HOW TO TRIGGER A LOVE-BOND

A love-bond can be triggered with the suddenness of a gunshot, and the aim is sometimes wild.

In Shakespeare's comedy *A Midsummer Night's Dream*, Lysander declares, "The course of true love never did run smooth." No wonder.

(Beware of love, and of the following paragraph, which you may have to read twice—but that's the point.) In the play, Demetrius declares his love for Helen, but then falls in love with Hermia and is granted Hermia's hand in marriage by her father. Hermia, however, is in love with Lysander and would sooner die or remain a virgin for life than marry Demetrius. Demetrius doesn't flinch at the insult and insists on marrying Hermia. Lysander, who at the opening of the play is in love with Hermia, runs off with her to the woods. However, in the woods, a fairy magically causes Lysander to fall out of love with Hermia and in love with Helen.

Helen has told Demetrius that Hermia and Lysander

have run off to the woods. Predictably Demetrius follows, and Helen follows Demetrius. Helen, pursuing Demetrius, makes the classic mistake of a forlorn lover—she begs:

> DEMETRIUS: Do I entice you? Do I speak you fair?
> Or rather do I not in plainest truth
> Tell you I do not nor I cannot love you?
> HELEN: And even for that do I love you the more.
> I am your spaniel; and, Demetrius,
> The more you beat me, I will fawn on you.
> Use me but as your spaniel—spurn me, strike me,
> Neglect me, lose me; only give me leave
> (Unworthy as I am) to follow you.
> What worser place can I beg in your love
> (And yet a place of high respect with me)
> Than to be used as you use your dog?

It would be almost impossible to love anyone who begged like that. In fact, when the fairy Puck causes Demetrius as well as Lysander to fall in love with Helen, not even Helen believes it. She assumes they are fooling her.

> HELEN: Can you not hate me, as I know you do,
> But you must join in souls to mock me too?

Helen, in her heart, as most begging lovers do, knows that begging, except perhaps for luck bordering on magic, cannot win a lover.

Part of the humor of the play arises from the apparent paradoxes:

> HELEN: O, teach me how you look, and with what art
> You sway the motion of Demetrius' heart!
> HERMIA: I frown upon him, yet he loves me still.

HELEN: O that your frowns would teach my smiles such skill!
HERMIA: I give him curses, yet he gives me love.
HELEN: O that my prayers could such affection move!
HERMIA: The more I hate, the more he follows me.
HELEN: The more I love, the more he hateth me.

The paradox is based on illusion. Begging may express the longing for a lover, but it does not demonstrate love. Helen's begging elicits its just reward.

Another part of the humor of the play arises from the unpredictable manner in which people fall in love with one another. The fairy's magic love drops are a metaphor of the seemingly irrational process of people falling in love.

Helen loves Demetrius, who loves Hermia, who loves Lysander, who at first loves Hermia in return, but then a fairy creates mischief, and suddenly Hermia is left in the lurch and Lysander and Demetrius are in love with Helen, but Helen can't believe anybody would love a pathetic beggar like herself and so assumes that she is being mocked by all.

There seems to be no basis for the magic-induced choice of lovers. The beautiful Titania, queen of the fairies, takes one look at an ignorant weaver whose head has been turned into an ass's head, and falls madly in love with him. Theseus, duke of Athens, declares in the fifth act:

Lovers and madmen have such seething brains,
Such shaping fantasies, that apprehend
More than cool reason ever comprehends.

Love can apprehend beauty in the most unlikely of persons, and in the likely the beauty apprehended is perhaps even greater. How can one trigger a love response like that?

The simplest and most direct method is by loving. Quiet, persistent, nondemanding loving by someone who also loves himself or herself is almost impossible to resist. In the following chapters we will demonstrate this method by taking our definition of love seriously. We will look at how a 100 percent commitment of active concern for the life and growth of the love of your life translates into action.

However, before you take action, before you are ready even to contact your lover, it is necessary to prepare carefully, to avoid the common mistakes that frustrated lovers make and prevent yourself from falling into the same destructive behaviors that pulled you apart.

PART II

Preparing for Contact

"If two people love each other there can be no happy end to it."
—Ernest Hemingway

or

"Love is . . . an ever-fixed mark that looks on tempests, and is never shaken."

—William Shakespeare

Chapter 3

STOPPING MISTAKES BEFORE YOU START

Are you about to make some big mistakes? The common mistakes that frustrated lovers make?

To help you avoid mistakes before they occur, I suggest you take the following quiz. Some of the answers may seem obvious, but strong emotion can blind us to the obvious. A little thinking ahead of time—before your next contact with your ex-lover—may help you avoid the obvious, and not-so-obvious but all-too-common, mistakes.

Circle *True* or *False* after each statement. After you have answered the quiz, read through the chapter, and at the end check your answers. I have deliberately designed scenarios in which lovers face multiple, interwoven issues, just as in real life you will often be faced with more than one issue at a time.

Common mistakes often occur not because people do not know what is wrong, but because in emotionally charged situations they haven't paused to think about what they do know. Much of the time psychotherapy helps people to become aware of or appreciate what they already know, so that they can act on their own wisdom. With this thought in mind, here's the quiz. (You will find the correct answers listed on page 61.)

TRUE OR FALSE?

1. If your ex-lover is seeing someone else, you should insist that your ex make a choice—the other person or you.
True   False

2. You should give high priority to finding out as much as you can about the competition, so that you will know what you're up against.
True   False

3. When you are not actually with your ex-lover, you should try not to think about him or her.
True   False

4. If your ex-lover talks about the competition, you should take the opportunity to point out why you are the better choice.
True   False

5. As long as your ex-lover brings up the subject of the other person first, you can then take the opportunity to honestly point out the incompatibility of the other person with your ex-lover.
True   False

6. You should imagine (or visualize) your ex-lover and "the other person" making passionate love so that you can get yourself used to the idea and it won't bother you anymore.
True   False

7. If your ex-lover talks about the competition, you

should, as politely as possible, ask her or him to change the subject.
True   False

8. If your ex-lover is regularly having sex with someone else and refuses to have sex with you, then your romantic bond has been dissolved.
True   False

9. Though in general, making demands is a bad idea, one thing you should demand is that your ex-lover spend at least some time with you.
True   False

10. If you can get your ex-lover to break a date with the competition, then you know you're winning.
True   False

11. Making your ex-lover feel guilt and pity can be a powerful method of manipulating an ex-lover back to you.
True   False

12. Sudden concessions—agreeing to what you previously opposed—for example, getting married, having children, or moving to another apartment, made after a lover has decided to leave you, are convincing demonstrations of love.
True   False

13. "But doesn't jealousy show that I care?"
True   False

14. Sudden attentiveness on your part for your ex *after* he or she has decided to leave may be a very unconvincing demonstration of love.
True   False

15. "I love you more than life itself" is a melodramatic but effective way of expressing love.
True   False

16. Emphasizing the intensity of your loneliness lets your ex know how much you miss him and therefore just how much you love him.

True   False

17. Though making demands for attention can be very risky, if your ex-lover gives in to your demands, that is evidence that you are succeeding in getting a lover back.

True   False

18. You should want your lover to spend time with you only if he or she enjoys your company.

True   False

19. Tell your ex-lover that you are willing to meet him more than halfway (say 40 to 60 percent).

True   False

20. If your ex-lover would help a stranger cross the street, he or she should at least *help you* deal with your loneliness.

True   False

Bob had been listening to heart-bleeding songs belted out by Neil Diamond. One of them, "Sweet Caroline," he especially liked because it sounded like "Marilyn," the name of the girl he had on his mind. They had been friends at first; they'd have lunch, or meet in the hallways at Frostburg State College. They commiserated over the nature of friendships, relationships, and the meaning of life. Marilyn listened sympathetically, her green yellow-flecked eyes trained upon Bob. Her voice had a soothing way of calming an anxious heart and drawing it toward her.

She was "going steady" with an athletic type who drove

a Datsun 300ZX, but she found it flattering that Bob sought and valued her advice, though at times he dwelled excessively on his heartache, causing her feelings to hover between gentle admiration and pity. Yet she was also in doubt about her feelings toward her "steady." Her feelings were in delicate balance, which is not to say she was consciously considering the idea of directing romantic attention toward her new friend.

As the friendship grew deeper, Bob told her in a sorrow-filled tone that he "felt socially cut off . . . not close to anyone."

She answered, as she pointed to herself, "Don't you feel close to me?"

"No, I feel cut off from you too. I . . . I . . ." His voice trailed off into vagueness.

"I feel close to you," she said. "I don't talk to other guys the way I talk to you. I feel closer to you than anyone else other than Jay. I think I've really gotten to know you, Bob, and even after knowing all this about you, I still like you— I guess I could say I love you."

He watched her eyes a moment, taking pleasure in the sound of her words and the color of her eyes, slowly recognizing the depth of his own feelings. "That makes me feel like crying."

"You do and I'll kill you."

They both laughed.

Now, if in the succeeding weeks someone could have intervened and told Bob to take things gently, perhaps something romantic could have developed. If he had paid attention, he would have been sensitive to Marilyn's need not to be pressured, would have been sensitive to her confusion about her steady, perhaps becoming her confidant. However, instead of taking the opportunity to become a special friend, he suddenly began making demands, became a distracting nuisance, calling too often, always happening upon the scene ready to discuss his heartaches and longings. To put it bluntly, he had become a mosquito she didn't have the heart to swat.

Bob turned her expression of love for him into a kind of accusation: "But you said that you loved me!"

Instantly she blamed herself for having said it. She hastily took back the unappreciated remark by turning her love into a generic equivalent: "I meant that I love you in the way I love everybody."

. . . *And the wind, and the rain, and the trees,* he thought sarcastically, too caught up in his own immediate longing to see the damage his insensitivity was doing to whatever potential they had of being something special together.

Bob greatly resented the existence of Marilyn's steady, the competition. He ridiculed him as "that jock," obviously someone who was beneath her level. He felt it was obvious that she was too intelligent and too sensitive for a jock. Pressed, he would have had to admit that he envied the jock's physical prowess—though he had never seen the man. He conjured up images of what he considered to be the competition. He wasted time and energy, tortured himself, increasing his anxiety and need by contemplating an athlete with whom he could not hope to compete. Whenever he saw Marilyn, his heart leapt. She could soothe his anxiety and make him feel whole. Yet he was oblivious to *her* anxieties and needs.

The day came when he screwed up his courage to take on what he considered the real issue and, in the process, screwed up his relationship with Marilyn. He sent her a 45-rpm record called *Change Partners.* He was determined to do the wrong thing (only dimly aware that he was, in fact, doing the wrong thing) and finally sent the record off to her with a card saying, "Just kidding, but . . ."

Two days later he got a message that she had called. He called her back.

"I got your record. Were you serious?"

"It's like the card said."

"Well, can I call you later?"

"Sure."

His phone finally rang. "Hello."

"This is Jay. Is Bob there?"

"This is Bob."

"Listen, you know Marilyn?"

"Yes."

"Well, I'm her boyfriend, and I am only going to tell you this once—I don't want you calling her, talking to her, writing her, or sending her any presents. As much as I love this girl, I don't want you bothering her. She's been trying to tell you to back off without hurting your feelings, but you've been too dense to get the message. If I have to, I'll break your neck."

"I don't care what you say, what counts is what Marilyn says."

The noise of phone movement on the other end, then, "Bob?" Marilyn's voice sounding the way it used to.

"Yes."

"I don't have time right now, okay? I'll see you in the fall at school." (That was two months away.)

"Okay."

Click. He was left with the silence of his room. She had given his number to Jay, and Jay had threatened to break his neck. How could she? He focused on his hurt, on the sense of betrayal. Could this be the same person who had told him she loved him? In a way he knew that he had made her regret having said it. He focused on his hurt, vomited, and cried. He was in no condition to win Marilyn back, or anybody else.

Bob focused on his own feelings, including the need he felt to push aside the competition, but the competition was not the issue. In fact, it turned out that Jay and Marilyn broke up several months later, but in the meantime, Bob had destroyed his friendship with Marilyn. In reality he was a poor friend, because real friends are sensitive to the needs of others as well as their own. His concern with Jay was totally beside the point. Jay's response to Bob indicated Jay's insecurity. Perhaps he sensed the coming end of his own relationship with Marilyn, and Bob gave him a target at which to aim his own frustration. She cared for him and perhaps for Bob as well. A little love directed toward Marilyn—active concern and sensitivity for what was going on within her—might have helped her sort out her feelings. Even after the damage was done, Bob might have "gotten her back" if he had known how to love her.

The message to take away from this story: The issue is not the competition; it is the ability to love. The best way to deal with competition is not to treat the person as "competition."

You could spend hours driving through the neighborhood to which your ex-lover has moved surveying the intersection of roads, the layout of the buildings, and, perhaps, the exact building in which your ex now lives. *There* are the very trees under which he or she must walk. Jealousy can envy even the trees and the sidewalk upon which your ex-lover must tread. Angry fantasies of revenge can fill the head. You can see it now as the apartment or house blows up. You sink into a depression. What would your ex-lover do if you killed yourself? That would teach him. He'd never be able to look his new lover in the face without feeling guilty.

Dwelling on the competition will result in grief and debilitating jealousy. Minor details—the person's eye color, cut of hair, talents, possessions—will take on undue but major significance. It makes you less effective when you finally share time with your ex-lover, because you'll have countless negative pictures dancing in your head. The self-torture of deliberately contemplated negative pictures (fantasies)—which may or may not have a basis in reality—increase anger and/or depression, both of which will interfere with your concentration when you attempt to create pleasant moments with the person you are trying to love.

The trappings of an ex-lover's new living situation are relatively insignificant, but they don't seem that way if you think about them enough. You may find yourself wondering if you should move into *that* neighborhood, rent an apartment like the one "the competition" has, buy a car like she has, and so on. When you get your lover back, all of these things will become insignificant. You do not need to imitate anyone. He loved you once. If you change yourself by becoming sensitive to your ex-lover's needs rather than imitative of the competition, then you will be better able to make effective use of any time, no matter how limited, you and your ex-lover have together. It is very difficult to have a pleasant time together if you are sick with jealousy.

Any attempt to imitate the competition will be obvious. It will be seen as manipulative, desperate, and pathetic. Manipulation (especially blatant manipulation) elicits anger. Desperation chases lovers away. Pity inhibits love. (You are attempting to nurture a spark of love into a flame. If your ex-lover feels pity for you, then you are trying to start a fire with a wet match.)

Dismiss negative images of jealousy from your mind. Use instead *positive visualization*. When you think of your ex-lover, visualize shared happy moments involving you and him, or visualize your ex with his friends or with his mother, but not with the competition. Do not reflect on the competition—such reflections need not and should not be present in the mirror of your mind. Positive visualizations make you stronger. Negative visualizations debilitate.

If you have prepared yourself, when your ex mentions the other person, you will be able to listen without pouncing. You may become her or his confidant(e). He can talk openly with you without being attacked, and once he starts confiding in you, you are more than halfway home. Odds are extremely unlikely that the competition will maintain the same equanimity. She probably immediately projects herself into your ex-lover's comments, points out your defects, argues with your ex-lover, and tugs at him, blatantly attempting to manipulate, and she therefore cannot be a good listener. Normally this would not do her great harm, because normally you would be making the same mistakes. (There would be the risk that if the tug-of-war became too severe, he might walk away from both of you.) If, however, you listen calmly, he will be drawn to you. You are less of a hassle. The process of thinking things out, of bringing tentative thoughts into the open to share with another, can occur only if one is not under attack. You can be the significant other who helps your ex sort out feelings. You are the one who listens and gently reflects back. You are the one who helps clarify. In doing this you will, in fact, *be influencing*, though in a nonthreatening, more subtle way. Not only your words but your calm behavior will have its effect.

Your ex-lover need only know that you love him or her totally, that you want to be the one who makes her happy, and that the really important thing for you is that she be happy. Say this occasionally, but resist the temptation to be repetitive. Repetition starts to sound like self-doubt.

Even if he says, "Oh, I don't know what to do. She wants me to move to _____ (someplace a thousand or more miles away) with her," you can say, "I don't know her. I can't say anything about her. I do know that I love you and want more than anything that it should be you and me, but you have to decide what you want to do. I hope you don't go, but I love you so much that if that's what you want to do, then you should do it." (Do not flinch when you say this. You are simultaneously being a good listener and utilizing what salespeople call the take-away.)

If, in fact, you do know his new lover, you can even point out her positive qualities to him (provided it doesn't ring false), gently adding that you, of course, love him and believe he will be happier with you but that he must decide what he wants. You will wait for him, you say. (He knows there are limits to how long you will wait. You could, in fact, come across a pebble on the beach that glimmers in the palm of your hand more brightly than he, but do not say this. To do so would be to threaten him. If you threaten, you are not loving, and remember, you are going to win him back with love.)

This approach will be much easier for you if you have prepared yourself with positive visualization. If once or twice a day you picture vividly in your mind what you most want to happen, it is more likely to happen. This is the positive side of self-fulfilling prophecy. If you have clearly in mind that you want and can imagine what you want actually happening, you will have the confidence that you need and you will be more likely to do what is necessary to achieve your goal.

Imagine a skier the moment before he begins a downhill competition. The light poles in each hand are poised to push off, then suddenly he tells himself, just as he pushes off, "This is not going to work." What do you think is going to happen? The effect is even worse if, along with the self-destructive thought, he *visualizes* himself tumbling in the snow. It is hardly magic to focus one's concentration on success instead of failure to give an added edge.

People can go their whole lives telling themselves, "This is not going to work." Need they be surprised when their self-fulfilling prophecy comes true? *Be aware* of your own thoughts and visualizations; they can determine the course of your life. What we tell ourselves can affect the outcome of our interactions with others, just as what a skier tells himself can affect his performance. For example, you ought not to tell yourself, "I don't deserve my lover," or even "My lover doesn't deserve me." If you do, you are programming your brain to cause you to act in accordance with those beliefs. You cannot, and should not, attempt to monitor all your actions—to do so will make you incredibly awkward, like an adolescent falling all over himself. Your every action is guided automatically by your underlying beliefs, so be very careful to examine your beliefs about yourself and your ex-lover, and be careful of what you visualize.

Positive visualization does not mean that one should live in a fool's paradise. Positive visualization, along with positive beliefs, help establish a mind-set that will help you relax and prepare you to take advantage of every opportunity to continue the successful living of your life. (For a detailed discussion of the effect on your life of what you tell yourself, see Shad Helmstetter's *What to Say When You Talk to Your Self.*)

If you lie awake at night picturing what you feel your ex-lover must be doing at that very moment, you just torture yourself. Your ex-lover may or may not be enjoying lovemaking with someone else, and even if he is, their lovemaking very likely has little to do with whether or not you get your lover back—these are factors beyond your control, except to the extent that you let such thoughts affect you. Banish them from your mind, replace them with positive visualization, and forget about what's-her-name.

THE MISTAKE OF INSISTING ON SEX

Despite all the evidence to the contrary, many people continue to see the presence or absence of sex as proof of the presence or absence of a love-bond. One of my clients in therapy complained to me of how his would-be fiancée insisted on sex regardless of his mood, and if there was no sex, she became more and more insistent, which decreased his interest all the more. Then she would cry and become explosively angry. His description revealed a woman who interpreted sex as the crucial evidence of whether or not she was loved. In fact, her would-be fiancé *had* begun questioning whether or not he wanted a relationship with her. She correctly perceived the uncertainty of their bond, but then incorrectly assumed that the sex she managed to have with him somehow improved the situation. At best it allowed her to delude herself. Sex for her was less an expression of love, less even an expression of lust, than an expression of an overwhelming need to be reassured. Her insistence made her less attractive to him, even when he was otherwise inclined to have sex with her.

Sex is no mark of ownership. That is why it is incorrect to waste time worrying about whether or not your former lover is having sex with someone else. Love and sex are no more synonymous than are love and a good meal. An intense sexual attraction can trigger a falling-in-love response, but *falling* in love does not last and is quite different from *being* in love. What counts is whether or not the nature of the relationship is a loving one; if it is, then everything is transformed—the quality of everything: sex, shared meals, and conversations. You are at far greater risk of losing your lover to someone who can meaningfully converse with your lover than you are to someone who has merely mastered sexual technique.

Within the context of a romantic love-bond, making love ought to be an expression of the strength and sensitivity of your love, and if it is, it will in fact help bond your lover to you. (See chapter 6, "A Precontact Look at Sex.") To insist on sex when your lover, for whatever reason, does not want it is an expression of insensitivity and weakness.

GETTING THE NIGHT HE INSISTED ON (AND BEGGED FOR)

Inge has spent the week with Zeke, but today, as agreed upon, she is with Matt. A part of Matt had wanted to tell her that if she didn't spend the week with him instead, then she should go to hell, but that was a small part of him. He realizes that when he and Inge were living together, he had, for a long time, practically ignored her. He had told her to date other people. He had created this situation himself. Now he feels lucky to see her at all. He wants to build up the number of their good times together.

Today has been very pleasant for both of them, and she is going with him this evening to the concert. Today she seems to be with him totally—her eyes are on his as they talk, attentive, just the way they used to be.

Then his world collapses. "You know, I won't be staying with you tonight," she says.

He says without emotion—the voice of a stone talking— "I thought you were going to stay here tonight."

"I was afraid you might think that."

The stone gets hot: "You mean, you're going to spend the night with him again?!"

"I told him I would."

"But I thought we were going to the concert!"

"I agreed to the concert but not to spend the night."

"I'm not talking about making love, you know. I just wanted to spend the night with you."

"Always what *you* want. You don't care what I told *him*."

The word *him* grates on Matt. She seems to speak as if he were a deity instead of a devil. "I don't care what you told that asshole."

"Don't call him names. You've no right to do that."

"My God, you're defending him! I'll call that asshole whatever I want to call that asshole."

"I won't listen to you, then."

"It's been five nights since I saw you!" he screams. "Five nights that have seemed like an eternity, and every night I toss and drink myself to sleep . . . in a sweat, trying not to think of you with *him* . . . and it's now our evening together and you want to go back to *him*." He spits out the last word.

"Stop shouting," she says. Her voice, as always when she is angry, becomes high-pitched. The pitch grates on his nerves even more. He wants to strangle her, to force her to stop being so stubborn.

His own voice drops. "All I wanted was to spend the night with you. I know you'll go back to him tomorrow." (He hadn't known that, but he convinces himself he did.) "But tonight, Inge! Tonight. Things were going so well today. I got my old confidence back."

"I know you did, but look at you now."

His voice rises again. "Puhleeze, stay with me tonight. Show me just once that you can say no to him." (Matt wants to win a tug-of-war.)

"But I don't want to say no to him. Do you want me to do something I don't want to do?"

"Do it for me, Inge!"

Her face is like an expressionless mask. She says, "All right. Have it your way." Inge feels manipulated and resents it. As a result she is irritable and now prone to see everything that Matt does in a negative light. Matt has insisted on winning a tug-of-war with Zeke and has thereby won a Pyrrhic victory over "the competition," since his goal of getting Inge back is farther away than ever. He has allowed himself to dwell obsessively on the experience of his own depression, outrage, and hurt, and as a result has cut off awareness of what is really going on inside Inge's mind. To the extent that he is aware of Inge, he is irritated by her real feelings. He is angry at her because she just won't feel toward him the way he wants her to feel. He shows no respect for her as an autonomous person, which is a very poor way for him to express his love.

Inge stays the night—curled up near the foot of the bed, most of the bed an empty space between them. She remains immobile and silent, finally perhaps asleep. *If she moves any farther, she'll fall off onto the floor,* he thinks. If he were to say anything, she'd probably say she'd prefer sleeping on the floor.

The next morning an emotional distance remains between them. She removes several dresses from the closet. She says she's going to be needing some of her old dresses. He feels the diminishing number of her things around the house to be an ominous sign. He is at first relieved to see that there are still a lot of dresses left in the closet, but then she says, "I ought to get rid of these. I'm not going to wear them anymore."

"Are you ever going to be putting dresses back into my closet?"

"I don't know, Matt. I don't know."

Matt's initial response to the realization that he does not yet have his lover back, like that of many a rejected lover, is to make demands. *Making demands* is a common mistake. Usually the first demand is that the lover not see anyone else. Such demands are pointless, unless one's lover sees them as a kind of reassurance that he is loved, but the need for that kind of reassurance indicates that something is seriously wrong with the relationship at a deeper level—one's lover does not feel loved, either because he is not loved or because of an excessive neediness. Therefore to get attention, he attempts to create jealousy and elicit demands because he experiences the demands as expressions of love. In such cases real communication has broken down. The solution is to give attention and express affection, but not to make demands.

Matt is forced to accept Inge's interest in seeing Zeke, so he backs off a little, making the demand only that she spend this particular night with him instead of with Zeke. When the demand doesn't work, he resorts to pleading and manages to evoke enough pity so that, though she resents it, she agrees to stay with him. She would feel guilty if she did not stay with him. Evoking pity and eliciting guilt are also common mistakes. Pity and guilt are ineffective glue when it comes to mending love-bonds.

Rejected lovers often jump back and forth, demanding and then begging and then demanding again, inevitably casting themselves as frantic, pathetic—sometimes dangerous—pests.

There is a fine line between touching someone's heart by a declaration of devotion and clutching at someone's heart to insist that devotion be responded to in kind. No one can be required to respond to love.

THREATS

Someone who pretends to love may masquerade her own neediness with declarations of love. When her declarations are frustrated, she may suddenly hurl threats at the person she claims to have loved. As despair alternates with hope, she may jump back and forth between "I love you" and "If I can't love you, nobody will."

Neediness masquerading as love has a way of revealing itself even in its declarations of love. "I love you so much, I'd cut off my own arm before I'd hurt you" is a thin veil to the rage beneath the surface, temporarily directed back at the speaker. I know of a case where that very statement was made by a man who later hired someone to harm the woman who refused to love him back. He would have been incapable of love, even if she had loved him.

Statements like "I love you more than life itself," "You mean everything to me," and "I couldn't open the door without you" may be all right as poetic exaggerations but, if meant literally, indicate that the speaker cannot tolerate rejection and therefore is potentially a threat to his lover, himself, and anyone else who happens to get in the way of his need.

We all know intellectually that threats chase a lover away and are counterproductive for anyone seriously interested in salvaging a relationship. But too often rejected lovers throw intelligence to the wind. (Sometimes threats actually work, but only if the threatened person is as "sick" as the threatener.)

There are other kinds of threats—the threat to harm the competition, which is sure to chase away any self-respecting lover, even if she isn't interested in that person.

Just as much of a threat is the kind, even more common, that is some variation on the theme "I can't live without you." The threat may seem to be aimed primarily at oneself, but in fact it is an attempt to extort love from someone by evoking pity or guilt. A natural sense of human decency may lead the person you've victimized with such a remark to help you out the same way he or she might help out someone who just fell in the street, but the help is not based on romantic love. Successful romantic love ultimately occurs only between equals. The strengths that make lovers equal may lie in different areas, but there can be no romantic love-bond if one is the source of love and the other is a basket case who cannot or will not function unless she is loved.

Because guilt and pity can be very powerful, suicide threats or attempts often do succeed in manipulating an ex-lover back, but since the "love"-bond has been held together by the threat of suicide, the relationship will tend to break apart again *unless* the threat is repeated or, at least, implied. A relationship based on emotional extortion may last a lifetime, but the bond involved is more accurately described as a "bind" and has nothing to do with love or happiness.

VIOLENCE

Manipulative suicide attempts or self-inflicted injuries demonstrate self-hatred. The rejected lover may actually be punishing himself for not being worthy of the one she loves. She has based her own self-respect on approval by another and as a result lives a vulnerable existence. True peace of mind can come only from self-respect, which arises from within. We all require approval, but the most important approval is that which we give to ourselves. Self-approval is a prerequisite for, not the result of, a genuine romantic love-bond.

Many people project their self-hatred outward. It is not surprising that just as people sometimes invoke romantic love to justify acts of violence toward themselves, they may do the same to justify violence (not merely the threat of it) toward others.

There is a strong current of machismo in many cultures

of the world that carries the male toward violence. In order to establish his claim on the woman he loves, a man must be ready to commit violence not only in order to protect her but also to turn away others to whom she may be attracted. He may even feel compelled to do violence to the woman he "loves" in order to hold on to her, at which point he may be demonstrating a kind of primitive mating behavior. Women, of course, may also engage in violence. The issue of violence is discussed further in chapter 10.

SUDDEN CONCESSIONS AND SUDDEN ATTENTIVENESS

Sudden concessions, made after a lover has decided to leave, are unconvincing demonstrations of love and may evoke pity or anger.

Sandy had always wanted marriage and children, she claimed. For years she doted on her boyfriend, Neil, a dentist. She served as his loyal and efficient dental hygienist/secretary in his office. He grew accustomed to her doting on him. She was beautiful, intelligent, and sexy, highly desired by many men. Her devotion to him encouraged his smugness, his sense of superiority and power. He took her for granted. Finally another man, exciting and attentive, came along, and she left. Neil was crushed. He couldn't believe that his worshiper was just not interested in him anymore. He pleaded with her. When he saw that she was serious about the other guy, he impulsively proposed marriage and children. He thought that would please her; after all, that was what she had always wanted.

She experienced these proposals as insults. "Why is it only now when I am leaving you that you want to marry me and have children?" Did he think she was so stupid that she couldn't see through his maneuver? Did he not see that by using marriage and children as a means of holding on to her, he degraded them, that what she valued so highly was being used as bait, that his assumption that she would jump at the bait was arrogant? And, finally, that marriage and children could only be meaningful if he *sincerely* desired them? If she were to accept his offer, she would always be wondering if he resented what he had agreed to. Her anger turned to pity as the desperation of his action became more apparent to her. He was no longer smug. Perhaps he deserved to be knocked off his pedestal (although she had helped to put him on it). As he continued to plead, she felt even more sorry for him. Sandy had been looking for a strong man to take care of her (which, by the way, in her case, meant that within her she felt she couldn't take care of herself) and she couldn't be attracted to a man who appeared to be as weak as Neil now did.

Concessions—and the more dramatic they are, the more this is true—are hard to take seriously when made during a moment of panic. Sudden expressions of attentiveness, also a kind of concession in a relationship previously taken for granted, may come across as insincere and desperate. This is tricky business. You want to convince your lover that you really do care, but to be really convincing, one must speak from strength. Strength comes from knowledge of what you are doing. Make sure that *you* believe in the concession before you make it. If you understand what is happening, it's easier to be calm about it, easier not to act out of panic. If Neil had slowly courted Sandy and then, once he started experiencing some success, proposed marriage and children, Sandy could have been loved right back to him.

What's worse, when your lover scoffs at your sudden major concession, you will tend to panic even more, perhaps making more concessions, expressing affection in a rising crescendo—all of this will strike your ex-lover as false, even insulting. Your ex-lover's indifference seems proof that he or she no longer gives a damn. Whatever the concession—the kind of car you drive, the place you live, the nature of your relationship—must not arise out of panic if it is to be experienced as an expression of your love.

If Sandy did accept concessions made out of panic, neither she nor Neil would be happy, and Neil would be setting himself up for future extortion—she left him to get something she wanted and got it, so the next time she wants something, she knows what to do to get it. Neil would likely develop the habit of expressing affection only when Sandy is about to leave, only when he is made to feel insecure. Fortunately for them both, Sandy had more self-respect than that.

WHAT THE COMMON MISTAKES HAVE IN COMMON

All of these common mistakes—*sudden concessions, sudden attentiveness, competing with "the competition," jealousy, negative visualization, making demands and ultimatums, insisting on sex, evoking pity, evoking guilt, threatening,* and even *becoming violent*—have in common a profound lack of love. When a rejected lover engages in them, he is contradicting what he says he wants to do most—to love. To love is to pay heed to the needs of the person you love. When you resort to the above tactics, you're focusing only on yourself. The object of that kind of "love"—whether or not there is any conscious thinking about it—is not going to experience being loved. Many rejected lovers engage in these common mistakes, and that is why so many of them do not get their lovers back.

THE ANSWERS

1-F, 2-F, 3-F, 4-F, 5-F, 6-F, 7-F, 8-F, 9-F, 10-F, 11-T, 12-F, 13-F, 14-T, 15-F, 16-F, 17-F, 18-T, 19-F, 20-F.

Chapter 4

HOLDING EMOTIONS AT BAY

The power of need and desire can stun and overwhelm the rational mind, causing a person to act against her own interests. It is important to be more than intellectually aware. It is important not to be surprised by your own feelings. In this chapter we will first take a look at a short scenario of someone who could not (or would not) control her response to her own emotions, then we will see, through two extended examples, how to cope with emotions when you're with your ex-lover.

THE WOMAN WHO WOULD NOT TOLERATE HER EX-LOVER'S "INGRATITUDE"

I reviewed the common mistakes of rejected lovers with a patient of mine. We discussed various encounters she had had with her ex-lover, examining how she could avoid the common mistakes in her own life. Then each week she'd come back for another session. She'd begin the session, "Well, I blew it again." When she was with her former lover, things would start out fine, but then she'd be flooded by her own neediness and anger. Rather than enjoying the conversation, she'd start telling him about her need to be with him, slipping ever closer toward the sarcastic remarks he had come to expect from her. Their encounters would deteriorate into episodes of name-calling. She explained that even while it was happening, she knew she was doing the wrong thing, but she couldn't help herself. Each time she was with him, her rational thinking was swept away by her emotions.

I suggested that she avoid seeing him at all until she could control her response to her emotions. Every negative encounter served only to increase the mutual hostility between them and drive him further away from her. She agreed. Yet she continued to obsess about him, sometimes making an excuse to call him up or to "accidentally" meet him—each time giving into the sway of her needs, never demonstrating love, not even demonstrating self-respect.

I explored the pattern of her previous relationships with her to see if the past could educate us about the present. It became clear that she had never really been in love with anyone. That she had always gotten involved with men she felt were inferior to her, to guarantee that they would need her (in reality to guarantee that they would always be there to meet *her need to be needed*). Yet inevitably she'd tire of them, unless they left her first, in which case she'd experience an intense grief reaction, because she felt rejected, not because her love had failed. Her anger kept asserting itself because she was enraged that an inferior could be so ungrateful. Though she still wanted to win him back, she finally recognized that she did not love him, did not even really respect him, and if the relationship were going to change, she'd have to do both. She had always avoided the company of men she respected, a clear indication that she did not respect herself.

Either way she went—to try to "win" him back or to find someone else—she was going to have to see past her need to be needed to the goal, assuming the real goal was to build a romantic love-bond. Keeping that goal in mind is essential when buffeted about by emotion. If you are driving in heavy traffic and suddenly see an accident ahead, you don't let go of the wheel and scream, you hold on firmly and guide yourself as best as you can. It's a lot easier to guide yourself if you've got self-confidence. If you respect yourself, you can allow yourself to love and respect someone else.

Sometimes holding the goal in mind can keep destructive emotions at bay. Alcoholics are taught to "think the drink through," that is, to think past the first twenty minutes or so of the pleasant high that they know comes with the drink to the misery they know always follows, and to contrast that with sobriety. Rejected lovers can use a similar technique: Think the moment through, past the emotional release of declaring need or anger, and the further alienation that that will entail, to the long-term goal of a mutually committed love-bond. Thinking the moment through takes practice, but with deliberate repetition, it will become a very useful habit.

Rather than being overwhelmed by your own feelings and blurting out whatever comes to mind regardless of the consequences—the way out-of-control romantics do—ask yourself three important questions:

1. Is what I'm saying more an expression of love or of need?
2. If an expression of need, will saying it improve understanding between myself and my ex-lover?
3. If I am saying this out of a need to ventilate, can my ex handle it and understand it?

(If you must express need or dependency, it might be best to tell your ex what you are doing—"I'm ventilating now. I do feel lonely at times when you're not around. It's just the way it is now." That kind of ventilating could even be endearing if done infrequently.)

It may seem that all your personal anguish and longing would instantly evaporate if only your ex knew the full intensity of your need. You can just imagine the relief if your ex would say, "I love you. I'm coming back. You're all I want or need in the world." But to bring your neediness out now is to sacrifice the possibility of long-term fulfillment for the transitory relief of emotional "gushing." Let emotions gush when you are alone.

The anger (and the hurt from which it springs) that you may feel at having been left by your ex-lover is not really the business of your ex-lover. It has to do with you. In chapter 5, "Lonely Times," we will look in more detail at techniques to cope with this hurt. The anger you may feel if an ex-lover is inconsiderate, even abusive, is another kind all together. It is a signal that you need to communicate more effectively and/or set limits on your lover. How this is done is explored in more detail in chapter 9, "Dealing with a Resistant Lover," and chapter 10, "Loving Impaired Lovers, and Why People Bother."

BEING COOL—MANAGING, FOR THE MOST PART, TO AVOID THE COMMON MISTAKES

Matt is driving a faded blue, rust-blotched Falcon. He fends off thoughts of Inge in a newer car, a shiny blue . . . He mustn't think of it, but he can imagine her sitting in a . . . He can't help thinking of it. He can imagine her sitting in a Zeke's shiny blue Volvo.

Inge told Matt to pick her up in front of the Art

Academy, and then they would go for lunch. Matt knows that she expects him to take Beretania Street, which passes directly in front of the Academy, but it's just as easy to take the back route through Makiki. Somewhere in Makiki—a residential area not far from the business district of Honolulu—Zeke lives, and now that Inge lives there, too, Makiki has taken on a magical, nightmarish aura, and Matt can't resist driving through, wondering which apartment building might be the one.

Matt knows where Inge will walk. He may be able to pick her up on the way. That might surprise her a little and demonstrate . . . he didn't know what. At least they would have a few extra minutes together. Again, the irony of it— he used to avoid spending time with her, this time he left early. *Timing demonstrates priorities,* he tells himself.

He sees her walking across the left-hand side of the bridge. He is in the lane closest to the median strip. He glimpses her face—it is grim and preoccupied. He honks and waves at her across the oncoming traffic. She looks up. The grim expression fades into mild perplexity. He has come from an unexpected direction. He points to the road that passes behind the Academy of Art, and that is where he picks her up.

"*Wie geht es Ihnen?* [How are you?]," he asks.

She smiles. "*Prima. Und dir?* [Fine. And you?]"

He has given up Italian, and for the first time in four years has begun sprinkling his speech with German. His every German word expresses interest in her, he feels, though the timing of his interest is a little obvious.

"What happened to your Italian?" she asks.

"I sold my books and records to Froggies [a used book store]." He laughs. "They gave me a dollar fifty for them."

"I guess the market demand has gone down," she teases him, but she does not object. She asks, "What about the Spanish course?"

"I sold that one too."

"I don't want you changing your life for me," she says.

"I'm just putting first things first . . . a matter of priorities."

"Sounds a little suspicious to me," she says, but her voice is still pleasant.

"In six months I'll be speaking German fluently."

"Uh-oh, I'm in for it now."

"The next time I overhear you talking with your parents, I'll know what's really going on."

She laughs. "And when is that going to be?"

"Oh, if we go to the mainland to visit them or something."

"What makes you think we're going to be going to the mainland?"

"Well, maybe it's the 'or something' then. Besides, I just want to be ready in case we do."

"Oh," she says blankly.

Trying to recover a playful tone, he says, "I am going to speak better German than you."

In mock fear, she says, "Don't learn German too fast!"

They have a German-style lunch. . . .

"This sauerkraut actually tastes good."

"It's bland," she says.

"What I mean is it tastes bland."

They both laugh.

"Matt, don't go pretending things just to please me. I don't like that. That doesn't make me feel good."

"I won't. I guess I could be saying I won't because that's what you want."

"You see, maybe we're trying to force something."

Panic flutters like a wild bird trapped in his chest. He speaks calmly, "I promise to be a little disagreeable from time to time."

She looks at him; her eyes crease with laughter.

He breathes a sigh of relief. He says, "Remember when we first met and you used to make me German dinners sometimes?"

"Yes. I stopped doing it because you never said anything."

"Well, I really, *really* liked them."

"You could have fooled me." There was a little resentment in her voice.

"I know I was being a schmuck. It was my fear of commitment that got in the way. You making me dinner like that was too much like being married."

"You!! What an insult! What made you think I wanted to get married? Is that my fault, you were reading things into it?"

He still doesn't know if he had been reading things into it, but he says, "I wish I had allowed myself to tell you how much I enjoyed it."

"That was a long time ago."

"I can still tell you now." He changes his tone a little. "I'll be honest with you—I never thought I would like sauerkraut."

"A lot of people don't, but that's because they don't make it right."

"Who would have believed it?" he asks. "Even my own mother didn't know how to make sauerkraut."

"Don't trick me into ridiculing your mother's cooking." Her smile returns. "I'll be honest with you too." She looks at him.

His heart sinks. Is she going to say something horrible?

"I don't really like German food," she says.

She suggests they have ice cream for dessert.

(By making suggestions where the two of them might go and what they might do, Inge is helping Matt create a pleasant moment. She actively participates in the creation of that moment. Her participation is a positive sign, because, in essence, she is helping him prove the viability of their relationship. Matt will have an easier time winning her back than if she were simply passively going along, if only he can keep his cool.)

Now they sit on the front seat of the car, turned slightly toward each other.

She is so close; she is right here. Damn it, why won't she come home with me? He resists the impulse to make demands.

He looks out the window toward the daylight sky.

"Did you see *der Mondschein* [the moonshine] last night?" he asks with an obvious American accent.

"That's cute." She laughs. "*Der Mondschein?* We were . . . I was wondering if it would break through the clouds and it finally did."

We were cuts him like a short-circuited electric knife. That *we* was not she and he, it was . . . He grits his teeth and tries not to cringe.

Calmly, but a little awkwardly, he says, "It was almost full. Tonight it will be a beautiful white sphere with dark etchings on it." He is holding his hand up, half-cupped, as though picturing where it will be.

"Yes," she says. "And did you know, you can see it move?" she asks excitedly. "We were looking at it through the telescope last night, and I actually saw it move."

His erect arm drops to the seat. He is overly conscious of his hand on the torn fabric of the car seat.

She says, "I can't wait to see the moon tonight."

He wonders if she is deliberately hurting him. *She's wishing herself away from me. Why can't she just enjoy this time with me now?* The impulse to protest comes close to the surface, but then . . . *To hell with what she does tonight. I can't control that. Right now she's with me.* If she is trying to hurt him, he understands. There used to be times when she wanted to share the moon with him and he deliberately avoided her and the moon.

The ice cream is done. She says, "*Zeit zu gehen.* [Time to go.]"

"Oh, all right," he replies, putting the key in the ignition.

"How did you know that?" She smiles in surprise.

"What?"

"How did you know what I meant?"

He laughs. Her attention focuses on him like a soft breeze that blows away anxiety. "In six months I'll be reading Goethe's *Faust* in the original."

"I'm impressed."

"That's the idea." Matt asks, "Will we go for breakfast next week?" Inge has off Fridays and Matt has no classes to teach on Friday mornings. Zeke works. Not that she won't tell Zeke. An invitation from Zeke would have priority.

"I guess it'll have to be Friday morning," she says, mocking consternation.

His thoughts won't leave him alone. *Did that mean she will be with Zeke on Saturday? That's a foregone conclusion, you idiot,* he thinks to himself.

"Earth to Matt, are you with us?"

"Oh . . . yes."

"Is it a date?"

"Of course, Friday morning is fine. That's what I said, Friday morning."

"You can let me out here."

He wonders why she doesn't direct him (allow him?) to leave her off in front of Zeke's apartment. Perhaps she doesn't want him to know where the apartment is. How dare she! Doesn't she know he can find it if he wants to!? Is she afraid he will? He can see himself doing it—standing at Zeke's door in the middle of the night, a deranged look on his face as he rings the bell and bangs fist against wood, insisting that all sexual activity within stop forthwith and forever! *That ought to get her back,* he thinks sarcastically, knowing the opposite would be true.

"What's wrong?" she asks. "You always seem worried and lost in thought."

Great. That's just how I want to seem to her, again bludgeoning himself with sarcastic irony. "Nothing," he says. "I'm looking forward to when we get together again."

Traffic whizzes by, the sound indifferent and irritating to him. No matter his own personal melodrama, the world goes relentlessly on.

"What are you thinking?" she asks. She has turned slightly in her seat and is facing him.

He detects a hint of pity that makes her voice softer than usual, seeming to fill her voice with affection. How tempting to twist tenderness into guilt, squeeze out a flood of pity. No matter that the flood would drown out genuine affection at least, for a moment, he might have her clasping him tightly to her.

"No," he says.

"No, what?"

"Nothing. It's just that it is always hard to separate from you."

"Would it be easier on you if we didn't see each other?"

"Of course not. You know that's not true."

He embraces her, and she embraces him in return. He has to count the seconds to keep from swirling into soft eternity and never letting go. He squeezes tightly, feels the pressure of her ribs against his arms and torso. At twenty seconds he relaxes his embrace, trailing his hands down her arms, then lightly holding her hands in his own.

He says, "It makes me happy to be with you."

"Then why don't you look happy?"

His eyes get misty. "The tears are just part of it. [He would be better off if they weren't.] The main thing is I . . . we had a pleasant lunch today."

"Remember that," she says. "Don't be sad. Think of the pleasant moments."

I hope you do that too, he thinks. It's as though she were reading his mind, or this book.

Is Matt being dishonest by not expressing his feelings of anger, hurt, and desperate longing? No, he is giving a higher priority to his love for Inge than to his need to ventilate his feelings. It would be presumptuous of him to dump these emotions on Inge. He might make her feel sorry for him, but what goal would that serve? Certainly not the goal of *loving* her back to him. Inge knows he cares. It's okay if she knows it makes him sad that she's not with him, but that's not what he is trying to communicate. He is communicating by demonstrating that he loves her— he has created a positive experience with her—which is the essence of loving someone. He has no right to expect her to come home with him yet because he has not yet won her back.

Now that she is out of the car and he turns on the ignition and enters the traffic, he can shout her name. At least he's not shouting at her. He can scream that he loves her, that he'd love to share his life with her.

DID SCARLETT O'HARA AVOID THE COMMON MISTAKES? WILL SHE GET RHETT BUTLER BACK?

By the time Scarlett O'Hara came to the realization that it was Rhett Butler she loved, he, after many years of waiting, had already given up. Scarlett's perennial interest in Ashley, her perennial rejection of Rhett's overtures, coupled with the death of their daughter, was too much for him to take. Rhett had already gone through his grieving over the loss of his true love and, deciding enough was finally enough, turned away from Scarlett with the same resignation with which a man walks away from the gravesite of a friend. The love-bond was dead, and it was just at that moment that Scarlett discovered that she wanted the love-bond with Rhett after all.

Coming dangerously close to panic, she asks, *"Then— then you mean I've ruined it all—that you don't love me anymore?"*

"That's right," says Rhett.

> *"But,"* she said stubbornly, like a child who still feels that to state a desire is to gain that desire, *"but I love you!"*
> *"That's your misfortune."*
> She looked up quickly to see if there was a jeer behind those words but there was none. . . . She looked at him with slanting eyes that burned with a desperate obstinancy. . . .
> For a moment she was on the verge of an outburst of childish wild tears. . . . But some remnant of pride, of common sense stiffened her. She thought, if I did, he'd only laugh; or just look at me. I mustn't bawl; I mustn't beg. I mustn't do anything to risk his contempt. He must respect me even—even if he doesn't love me.
> She lifted her chin and managed to ask quietly:
> *"Where will you go?"*
> There was a faint gleam of admiration in his eyes as he answered.

A spark glows among the ashes. Perhaps the love-bond is not totally dead. He talks of what he wants from life now.

> *"I want the outer semblance of the things I used to know. . . . When I lived those days I didn't realize the slow charm of them."*

She remembers Ashley's words on the same subject, and says, almost accidentally placing her finger on Rhett's soul: *A glamor to it—a perfection, a symmetry like Grecian art."*

Rhett is startled. He *said sharply, "Why did you say that? That's what I meant."*

"It was something that—that [her stutter indicates she knows that what she says next is the wrong thing to say] *Ashley said once, about the old days."*

He shrugged and the light went out of his eyes.

The name Ashley irritated an old wound. Wounds take time to heal. He states with a calmness and seeming finality that is frightening to a lover: *"What is broken is broken. . . . My dear, I don't give a damn."*

He has loved her; she is now beginning to understand him. She is struggling against falling to pieces. She sees the importance of holding on to dignity—that is very important. She will retreat to Tara to find a way to meet her own needs—and plan a strategy. *She could get Rhett back. She knew she could. There had never been a man she couldn't get, once she set her mind upon him."* (Margaret Mitchell, *Gone with the Wind,* pp. 1,020–24.)

Though I don't mean to belittle what I believe to be one of the major points of *Gone with the Wind*—Scarlett's lack of concern about those around her has caused herself, as well as others, a great deal of anguish and rendered her oblivious to all that does not glitter—Scarlett demonstrates the basic insights needed to get her lover back. She has demonstrated throughout the book an uncanny insight into the psychological makeup of those around her, especially when that insight has anything to do with the goals she sets for herself. She understands the necessity of putting her own emotional panic and needs on the back burner when these would otherwise interfere with her goal. Therefore, the evidence indicates that she will be able to use her insights into Rhett's nature—now that she cares about Rhett's nature—to love him back to her (or to manipulate him back, if you think she is incapable of love). She is not likely to repeat mistakes she made in her pursuit of Ashley.

All along she has had a much clearer insight into Rhett than she has had into Ashley. Her idea of who Ashley was existed only in her mind. When she realizes that Ashley does not even remotely measure up, her desire for him vanishes with the fantasy. There is not even the excitement of a challenge anymore.

The most important insight that she lacked was insight into herself; she understood others and used that knowledge to manipulate. At last she is making discoveries about herself—one is the importance of Tara and the Old South to her, another is that she loves Rhett. When she sees that she has lost her hold on Rhett, she makes dramatic statements, but she does not fall to pieces. She is not likely to make the common mistakes rejected lovers often make. She does not beg. She does not throw an angry tantrum. She sees past the pain of the moment to her goal of getting Rhett back. Her words, as she quotes Ashley, zero in on what's important to Rhett, demonstrating the understanding that goes with love. The mistake of mentioning Ashley is a momentary misfortune. She understands Rhett, and she finally shows the emotional self-discipline to act on her understanding. Beyond that, she appears to be moving independently in the same direction as Rhett. Their hopes and dreams are similar, they seem to be a perfect match. The likely outcome of a sequel to *Gone with the Wind* is obvious. Frankly I don't think Rhett has a chance of resisting her.

In both of the extended examples in this chapter (the real-life one of Matt and Inge and the fictional one of Scarlett and Rhett), we have seen rejected lovers avoid mistakes by controlling their outward response to their inner emotional turmoil. They have given priority to the goal of getting a lover back.

Thinking through various situations in which you might be tempted to make one of the common mistakes and considering alternative courses of action before you make contact will make your chances of re-forming a love-bond much stronger and will help you keep your emotions from taking control.

Chapter 5
LONELY TIMES

While you are preparing to make contact, and then while you are working to win your lover back, you will be struggling with many intense emotions. There are several ways to deal with these and prevent them from ruining your attempt to win your lover back. We have already discussed the importance of controlling your response to these emotions when you are with your lover. Your ability to do so will be greatly enhanced if you learn to uncover and understand your emotions and ventilate them in private.

It is important to remember that "controlling" your response to emotions does not mean that your emotions, even negative ones, should be ignored. This chapter will deal with methods of coping with intense emotions in a way that will enhance the chances of getting your lover back.

It is not enough simply to avoid the food, the drink, the drugs that you may be tempted to use to fill the awful pit of loneliness. Without alternative ways of coping, avoidance of negative impulses is impossible. Nor can you simply grit your teeth and bear the feelings of unworthiness, fear, and uncertainty, so let us look at other ways of spending your time.

SCHEDULED REFLECTION

The bedroom, especially, can become an instrument of torture to a rejected lover. It reminds you, perhaps more than any other place, of what you had, what could have been, and of what you have lost. Usually here is where the closest intimacy took place, not just sexual but all forms of intimacy. Moods were less masked. Your hair was let down. You saw your lover and your lover saw you in the vulnerability of sleep. Probably you sensed each other's presence even in dreams.

Often, after a breakup, you still sense the presence of your former lover . . . reaching over to touch the person who used to be there, who you hallucinate in your dreams *is* still there. That's why waking up in the morning can jolt you with the cold, nightmare reminder of "My lover has left me"—depression with a bite. That's why it can be so sad and irritating when you come home alone to your bedroom.

The silence of being alone, even if there is noise of some kind, remains. And even if you bring someone with you to pass the time, the aloneness doesn't quit. Sexual pleasure or the pleasure of conversation can be felt, but it is distant and at best transitory. The wave of longing, momentarily pushed back by sex, conversation, or other amusement, returns with a forceful flow to the empty place in the middle of the chest.

So what do you do? Do you pursue amusement anyway? Do you date someone else? Perhaps, but first allow yourself to recognize and express your grief, at least to yourself and, as we will see in more detail later in this chapter, maybe to someone else. When something bothers you, it is a self-destructive act to deny it. The bother will continue just below the surface and explode to the surface at the wrong moment, getting you in trouble at work or interfering with loving your lover back to you.

I have said that it is important to give priority to your love-bond, but that does not mean that you deny the reality of your own feelings, including dependency, anger, and neediness. If you deny the existence of negative feelings, even to yourself, you won't understand your own actions. Acknowledgment of the presence of your feelings will provide at least a degree of relief and a lot of self-understanding. Acknowledgment does not mean acting out. It's simply saying to yourself, "Yes, that's how I feel. I feel that way because I miss my lover," and so on. If these feelings intrude at an inappropriate time, at work, for example, then think, "Yes, that's how I feel. I'll think about that later."

Make sure you do think about it later. In time you will be less bothered by intrusive, inappropriate thoughts and feelings during the course of the day, so long as there is a time when you allow them to be appropriate. At a time chosen by you, you can write notes, obsess, talk out loud to yourself, protest to the indifferent stars, cry in the shower or into your pillow.

Setting aside a time each day, say ten to thirty minutes each morning and ten to thirty minutes each evening to think over what you have done and what you plan to do, to allow yourself to feel and to think about what you have felt, is a good strategy for life, even if you are not trying to get your lover back. In times of stress, like just having been rejected by a lover, it's an especially helpful strategy. There is an analogy here with prayer, the kind of prayer that each night reflects on the day's activities and each morning visualizes how you wish to spend the day.

In scheduled reflection you do in a controlled manner what frustrated lovers do endlessly. You think about your lover. You fantasize yourself with your lover. You ruminate about conversations and interactions you had with each other, imagining what would have happened had you said something else, had you been—literally or emotionally— in another place.

During your scheduled reflection it may also be helpful to remember the bad times. Rejected lovers tend to cause themselves unnecessary pain by overromanticizing what they have lost. This is the result of dwelling just on the good times, altogether forgetting about the bad times. The best way of getting a lover back is to remember what really happened, remembering the bad times as well as the good times, the things you didn't like about your lover as well as the things you liked, so that when you say, "If only it could be like that again," you know what you are talking about. Only then can you make the good times even better and learn to minimize the bad.

If it turns out that your love is no more than a romantic fantasy, then a little reality-based remembering may result in your not wanting your lover back. If you *do* want your lover back, remembering the negatives will help you put things into perspective and deintensify grief. A balanced memory can lead to lonely nights that are a little less lonely, and there is nothing wrong with that.

NOTES TO YOURSELF

The longing, the desires, the neediness within the heart can sometimes be expressed through private writings. These feelings *should* be expressed in some way. Alone, in your room at night, you have an opportunity to bring them out without censorship, to grieve creatively.

You can write notes in a journal, a diary, or put scraps of notes in a well-hidden shoe box, pouring out every thought and feeling without restraint. Try it. Try to express as accurately and as clearly as you can what you feel and think about your life. At first you may feel frustrated that you are not quite writing it the way it is, but in time you will get better at it. You will become better not just at expressing what you feel but at getting to know your feelings, and then you can reflect on them and what they mean.

When you read back over what you have written, you will begin to notice patterns and will perhaps become aware of how some of these patterns lead to frustration. Each night as you write, you will notice the repetition of these patterns in what you describe, and, if you like, you can begin to change.

Although you may address your notes to your ex, you ought not show them to him. This is one time when you write for you. The primary purpose is different from when you communicate with your lover. You are trying now to understand your own feelings. Resist the impulse to use these notes, by inadvertently leaving them to be found, as a way of demonstrating the intensity of your feelings—there are other ways of doing that that are less likely to be guilt and pity provoking, as we shall see in later chapters. You need these notes for yourself.

The ventilation of feelings is an important part of writing notes to oneself. Describe your longing in all the purple details. There is nothing wrong with crying over your pages. You may find yourself writing poetry, songs, short stories, or even a novel, or just plain notes, but as long as you write for yourself and no one else, then you will be successfully using your "shoe box notes" to grieve creatively. As a result, in time, there will be less of a tendency to allow your own neediness to defeat you in your efforts to get your lover back.

The tendency to want to "accidentally" show your ex your secret notes before you have him back can be very strong, despite the risk of negative consequences. Don't do this. The notes are the place you put feelings too intense, too needy, too selfish for your lover to see. They are for *you*, not your lover.

After you and your lover are *definitely* back together, then, since you are no longer acting under the pressure of unfulfilled needs, the notes from your time of grief could become an expression of affection. Not only will they be flattering, they will carry the added weight of genuine love, for you did not show them to your lover when they would have been a momentary relief to you.

A SAMPLING OF "SHOE BOX NOTES"

These notes can vary in length, from a word (perhaps your ex-lover's name or a word describing a feeling: "sad," "horny") to many pages. They're not required to be of literary quality but ought to be honest expressions of thought and feeling.

3-21-85
(very early A.M.)

I just woke up from a dream in which my older brother, my sister and I were about to talk to my father in the "back office." My father wanted to know, "Where's all your students, Matt?"

I feel Inge's presence. I wake up and it immediately hits me that I miss Inge. I want her to be a permanent part of my family. More than anything I have ever wanted, I want to marry Inge. I feel bonded. Does she not feel it too? When will this strange separation end? I will always treasure her presence.

Comment: It might be better for Matt not to show this note to Inge even after he gets her back, unless he's really sure he wants to get married or unless the subject of marriage is not really as important to her as a genuine love-bond with Matt, assuming, of course, she wants a love-bond. In either case, until he gets her back, it would be premature to suggest marriage.

By the way, the dream can be rather straightforwardly interpreted: His students (Matt is a teacher) are symbolic of the children he and Inge could have had but are missing now as a possibility because Inge has left the family. His feeling that he wants to marry her, expressed in the paragraph immediately following the dream, logically follows, though at the time he wasn't aware that it was an explanation of his dream. Matt later described the feeling of the dream as one of "sad longing," a feeling that also fits the interpretation.

3-25-85
4:55 A.M.

I am sad because Inge is not here. She will come back, but every moment without her is like an eternity. Little things cut my heart—her black and white picture is missing. Little things give me joy—her toothbrush is still here. Does that mean she will be coming back? I love her still.

—M.

Comment: A nice message (ventilation) to oneself. Something to look back on at a later date, and one day,

when he has got her back, perhaps a touching note to
show Inge.

3-21-85

What frightens me is I see what happiness there
would be if Inge came back. Is such happiness allowed?

Comment: A recurring theme in some of Matt's notes is
this negativistic question, Is happiness allowed? Eventually
he realized the negative implications of it and learned to
say more positive things to himself.

A hidden belief that one does not deserve happiness, or
that happiness is not allowed, is the foundation of many
an unhappy life. In psychotherapy one of my first actions
is to ferret out such beliefs and expose them to the
conscious mind so that they can be disposed of and replaced with more positive beliefs. Happiness doesn't just
happen. There must be a belief that you deserve to be
happy so that you can then direct yourself toward the
goals that make you happy, including the goal of making
a relationship work.

A sad, vulnerable woman writes reassuring notes to
herself. The self-doubt is just below the surface. Her lover
left her about six weeks ago . . .

Sometimes there is a calmness in my heart. I know
that he is coming back to me. When he does, he may
even say that in our hearts we both knew it all the
time. When we are back together, just as we knew it
would be, that will mark the beginning of our life
truly spent together.

All I must do is wait. It is painful. Waiting is not so
painful really when I remember that I wait because I

love him. He asked me to be patient. He loved me patiently for so long. Why did I hesitate? Now it is my turn to wait patiently for him.

Music we once listened to is playing just now. The warm glow of our day together is still with me. We had lunch together today!

Comment: It is okay to be vulnerable in a shoe box note. There's another advantage to these notes. When you get your lover back, *you* can look them over. You can remind yourself how much this relationship meant to you when it seemed you might lose it. When you get your lover back, you can breathe a sigh of relief and, remembering how much your lover means to you, you can love him or her all the more, never falling into the trap of taking your beloved for granted.

One more example, written by the fictional character Charles in *The French Lieutenant's Woman* after his lover has disappeared on him:

O cruel seas I cross, and mountains harsh,
O hundred cities of an alien tongue,
To me no more than some accursed marsh
Are all your happy scenes I pass among.

Where e'er I go I ask life the same;
What drove me here? And now what drives me hence?
No more is it at best than flight from shame,
At worst an iron law's mere consequence?

Comment: This is fine as a shoe box note. Unfortunately for Charles, when he finally met up with his ex-lover again, he said, in essence, the same comments directly to her, evoking pity and maybe guilt in her—feelings that, as we learned in our discussion of common mistakes (chapter 3), are not conducive to romantic love.

TO HAVE A CONFIDANT OR NOT TO HAVE A CONFIDANT

Another tactic to use on lonely nights and at other lonely times is to share your thoughts with a confidant. But be careful. A confidant, a combination good friend and good listener who has your interest at heart and understands what your goals are, is hard to find.

If you wish a friend to become a confidant in the matter of your getting your lover back, state your wish to your friend in advance. Do not set up pseudosocial events that then become *your* therapy sessions. That would be friend abuse. It is natural enough to see the world through the eyes of your own personal grief, but your friends and acquaintances continue to have their own concerns. Healthy relationships of any kind require give-and-take; otherwise your friends may come to feel used, and you will find yourself friendless as well as loveless. If you want someone to be your confidant, ask him clearly and directly in advance. Warned in advance, your friend will not feel used. Remember, your friends have a right to set limits on what they will do for you. Do not pressure someone into the role.

Make certain you pick someone who has the maturity to keep a confidence. The last thing you need is for your special concern to become a public joke—your ex-lover will feel betrayed, and you will be less likely to succeed in reestablishing your love-bond.

Pick someone who is attuned to your goals and plans. (You ought to show him or her this book.) She can help you through difficult moments when you are tempted to put need before love. You might even come to an agreement that at moments of duress you can call your friend to ventilate your feelings and thereby avoid the need of calling your ex-lover. (This is analogous to the sponsor program in Alcoholics Anonymous. When an alcoholic is tempted to drink, he can call a sponsor to help talk himself out of the compulsion.) Overdependency on a confidant should not become a problem, as long as you are doing the other things recommended in this book.

Your getting-your-lover-back sponsor should not only be someone you can trust, he should be someone who believes in the basic idea of this book. Many people have learned to believe that there is more than one fish in the sea, and if your lover has left you, the best thing to do is to catch another fish. Such a believer is not a compatible sponsor.

Many people have experienced failed relationships, and the wrong kind of sponsor—one not really wanting to be made aware of the errors in his behavior that resulted in *his* own dissolved love-bond—may resent the possibility of your success. Such a sponsor may not be consciously aware of his own motivation and may actually believe he has your best interest at heart. Steer clear of well-meaning, self-righteous souls who have a need, subconscious or otherwise, for you to fail.

Ideally the best sponsor of all would be a person experienced in the art of making relationships work, one who cares for you and perhaps has saved his or her own relationship.

If you decide to pay for your sponsor by going to a professional counselor, make sure that your counselor understands your goal—show him or her this book. Counselors have their own hang-ups, so exercise caution.

Finally, a confidant is only an aide, perhaps a very

helpful aide, but if there's no one available, you can still get your lover back on your own.

IS IT OKAY TO DATE SOMEONE BESIDES YOUR EX-LOVER?

Yes, but . . . it is a bad idea to deal with lonely nights and other lonely occasions by allowing someone to fall in love with you when in your heart your commitment lies elsewhere. To do so is symptomatic of a profound lack of concern for others, and someone so lacking is by definition incapable of sustaining genuine love over time. Love is not just how you treat a particular person, it is an attitude toward the world.

There are those who will insist that they love only one person and the rest of the world can go to hell. Cutting off the world, widening one's ego just enough to include two, makes for an intensely dependent relationship. The intensity of need in such a relationship is often mistaken for love when it is actually an impediment to love. Unless sensitivity for others is nurtured as a way of life, then, even within the world of two, superficial fondness will be pierced again and again by resentment. An underlying cynicism will destroy the love-bond, replaced by an addiction-bond that is held together by the fear of being alone.

The point of view that loving must be the way of relating to life if there is to be any love, including romantic love, is an interesting philosophical theme. You could read more about it in Erich Fromm's *The Art of Loving,* but for the purposes of this book, suffice it to say that in your attempts to get your lover back, you ought to treat everyone in a caring manner. Maybe you don't believe it's necessary, but I recommend you do it anyway. You owe it to yourself. Otherwise, any success you experience is going to be temporary. For the virtues like caring for others are virtues because ultimately they are the most effective way for people to live.

So, the virtues aside, I'm saying it's okay, maybe even a good idea, to date someone else during your campaign to get your lover back, so long as you are honest about what you are doing. If the person seems to be getting serious about you, or your new relationship is starting to take on the quality of a romance, then it's important to let the person know what else is going on in your life.

How soon should you start dating? If your lover has recently left you, consider waiting awhile. He or she may be coming back to you soon. Give yourself a chance to use some of the approaches in this book. Sometimes response is very rapid. To suddenly be dating someone else could confuse the issue. It is true that some people successfully pull their lovers back into a relationship by dating someone else to create jealousy, but that kind of success is short-lived and is not love-based.

Naturally if you've got time on your hands and your lover is not back with you yet, and may or may not be involved with someone else, you're going to want to socialize, especially if you've got your grief reaction under control. In fact, socializing will help you get it under even better control. So, you go out. At first, perhaps, with a group of friends. Later maybe with a date. If your ex-lover wants to know where you were and who you've been with, you matter-of-factly tell her. Don't flaunt it, don't go into details even if asked to do so. You love your ex-lover and you want to spend time with her or him, but you're going to continue with your life. If your ex tries to make an issue out of this, hold your ground. Later, in chapter 9, "Dealing with a Resistant Lover," we'll discuss how to handle disagreements and unreasonable anger. If your ex is seeing someone else, it is okay for you to spend time with friends, including your own someone else. But never, never use this as a threat. You love your ex, but you are also a normal human being who needs a social life.

PURSUING YOUR OWN INTERESTS

If you decide to date, let your dates know in advance—especially if there are any signs of romantic interest—that you are involved in a serious relationship with someone else, the outcome of which is not yet determined. In addition to the reasons already discussed, you will be heading off the potential complication of a hurt would-be lover showing up when your ex-lover returns.

You date if you feel like dating. Regardless of whether or not you feel like it, you ought to socialize with friends and acquaintances occasionally. This will head off inordinate dependency on your ex—your social needs will already be met, you won't *need* your lover for that.

By the way, people who don't socialize become socially "rusty" after a while. It actually becomes more difficult for them to talk and relate to others. Socializing is a kind of exercise that you need to do if you're to retain the ability. I have seen cases where people became so caught up in their own grief that they withdrew from social life altogether, and when they attempted to return, they felt awkward, out-of-step. They were not sure how to relate anymore and wondered what they looked like to others, which led to "self-spectatoring," as when someone is so busy watching himself bounce a basketball that he can't bounce it. Social "rustiness" can get in the way when you finally start spending time with your ex again. In extreme cases, social withdrawal may lead to panic attacks and agoraphobia when a person attempts to reenter the world of human beings. Socializing and activity have been demonstrated, in a controlled study, to prevent depression. Obviously you will be better able to love if you are not depressed.

Activity includes physical exercise. We will discuss, in chapter 6, the importance of exercise to keep the body in shape, but there's another aspect to it. Physical exercise helps the mood. The body starts pumping peptides of well-being, such as endorphin, into the blood. You've got more energy, more color, you feel ready to take on challenges with these exercise-induced hormones in your blood.

Your exercise could be in the form of a new sport, tennis, racquetball, hiking with the Sierra Club, or even jumping rope. Social exercising is a great way of meeting friends and fending off loneliness.

In chapter 7 of the book *Jump into Shape,* by Sydney Filson and Claudia Jessup, "The Social Jumper," we come across a case in point:

> If you are lonely and would like to find a friend, take your jump rope somewhere, anywhere! If you jump rope near other human beings, you are bound to make new friends. It's a good bet that someone you attract while jumping will say, "Hey, I used to be pretty good at that. May I try your rope?" The full bloom of nostalgia has taken over. Hardly anyone can resist the urge to flash back to childhood.
>
> It's funny. People who normally would never speak to strangers—let alone ask to borrow from them—will zero right in on your rope.

Similar things can be said for other forms of exercise. If your former lover is also exercise conscious, you have something new you can share. When my ex-lover became my lover again and we went apartment hunting, I noticed a pool and said, "I'm going to teach you how to be a professional-class swimmer in that very pool." She smiled.

You can also pass the time and socialize by taking a day or evening course in an interest you always meant to pursue—foreign language, music, or even a science class. The more interests you have, the more interesting you are.

PART III
Getting Back Together

"Come live with me, and be my Love;
And we will all the pleasures prove."
—Christopher Marlowe

Chapter 6

A PRECONTACT
LOOK AT SEX

While you and your lover are apart, you have an opportunity to escape patterns of behavior that may have become ingrained. This is a good time to evaluate how sex was between you and whether anything might be changed. Bad sex can seriously damage an otherwise healthy love-bond. Rarely is sex alone *the* problem in a relationship, but it is often a source of stress in a relationship with problems.

WHAT IS BAD SEX?

If there's good sex, a lot of things can go wrong before a lover will give up on a love-bond. Good sex is not sufficient to create a love-bond, but it will help strengthen and mend a romantic relationship gone bad. Bad sex will tear a relationship apart. Sex is communication on a physical level; bad sex is bad communication. Bad sex means that lovers are out of touch with each other, are on different wavelengths. Occasionally being out of touch is an understandable human failing, but being out of touch in the long term spells the end of a relationship.

What is a relationship anyway? Two people come together. They possess the prerequisites of a certain amount of self-esteem, a curiosity about life, an awareness of a desire to share life closely and intimately with each other. That sharing involves many things. In a romantic relationship two people learn to love each other. They gain knowledge of each other, of potentials, of desires, of weaknesses and strengths. This knowledge is made possible by communication—verbal communication, body language—gestures, facial expressions, posture, affectionate touching, and sensual, passionate touching (including smelling, tasting, listening, and feeling). All avenues of communication strengthen the relationship-bond, and when romantic love is present, sex, the passionate physical form of communication, strengthens the love-bond, and it feels good, and the better it feels, the more reason lovers have to share each other's company.

WAS BAD SEX YOUR PROBLEM?

Sometimes lovers stay together because of sex alone. More likely, if there's trouble in a relationship, there's trouble in communication, including sexual communication. Bad sex means a breakdown of communication and involves two people. It is not important whose fault it is; it is only important that communication be improved. Communication can't be improved if you're not willing to look at the possibility that it might need improving. You can start the improvement. If you're trying to get your lover back, you can't play the "he's got to try too" game.

You're by yourself with your thoughts and this book. No one is going to point a finger at you. Ask yourself the

question, Was sex with your ex-lover good? Did you enjoy
yourself? Were you spontaneous? Relaxed? Were you sensitive to your lover? How do you know? Did you ask? Did
you try different techniques? Did you take pleasure in
giving pleasure? Did you vary the style? How do you know
who likes what if you don't try different things and if you
don't talk about it? Grunts and groans, though informa-
tive, can often be misleading, or even faked.

Often people don't even know what they themselves
enjoy most until by accident or by experimentation they
discover it. Lovers are in an excellent position to become
especially good at sexually loving one another, because
they have the time to get to know each other's bodies, to
experiment and make discoveries. Unfortunately, they
sometimes throw away this advantage by settling into a
boring routine, which they may continue out of a sense of
sexual duty or because as Woody Allen once said, "I never
had an orgasm I didn't like."

A woman was in psychotherapy with a common problem—an unsatisfying sex life. Her husband didn't realize
it, but he would soon be in need of my advice on how to
get her back if communication between them didn't improve soon. They were having sex but she was never
coming to orgasm. Like 60 percent-plus of the female
population, in order for her to reach orgasm, she would
require direct manipulation of her genitals by fondling,
oral sex, or a vibrator. This required informing her husband about what pleased her. She was hesitant to inform
him for fear of offending his sensitive male ego. She was
building up resentment at being left frustrated by her
lover, who smugly assumed that since he was satisfied, she
was. Unfortunately she, like many women in such a predicament, went through the appropriate moans and groans
to play to her mate's delusion. So she became increasingly
irritable, looked forward to lovemaking less and less, and

picked fights over many issues that had nothing to do with sex. Bad communication on the physical level was leading to bad communication all around.

She came to recognize the negative pattern she was in. Finally, after much hesitation, overcoming her fear of offending her partner's maleness, she had a talk with him. With a little education, he became a good lover for her. She didn't have to pretend anymore. Learning to communicate sexually provided a lesson in learning to communicate in general. The fact that he was able to listen bodes well for the future of their relationship. He is willing to learn. He did in fact have a lot of the paradoxically delicate sensitivity of the macho male, but his love overcame that failing. It would have been sad had it been otherwise—he and she would have lost a chance to grow together.

Mental health workers are well aware that even in post-sexual-revolution America, most men and women have difficulty talking about sex, even in the privacy of their own bedrooms. There is incredible emphasis placed on sex in our culture, and yet incredibly enough, ignorance and a lack of communication about sex continue to be commonplace.

Not talking about sex leads to bad sex. If you claim to love someone romantically, you owe it to your lover and to yourself to work through any hang-ups you have in the area of communication. If you can talk about sex and can sensitively lead your ex-lover to talk about it with you, you are more than halfway there to getting your lover back. I can say this because if you can talk about this subject, which can be so difficult, you will also be able to talk more openly about other important subjects.

If your ex-lover is still physically present, you can bring up the subject. You know your ex-lover best; I cannot tell you exactly how to do this. You will be safe, however, if you remember not to *force* a discussion. Let your ex know that you would like to talk about sex. If refused, you remain open to talking about it if your ex would like to. Do not criticize. Your purpose is to love, and to that end, you wish to communicate so that you can both learn and grow. If this is an especially sensitive area for your lover, then all the more reason to go slowly, giving your ex-lover the feeling that you will not pressure him to talk about things he is not ready to talk about and that you are not out to criticize or be criticized but that you do want to learn.

You might borrow an approach I use in psychotherapy. Often there are subjects people find difficult, even painful to talk about. The fear of being overwhelmed by the pain of their own emotions can lead people to be very resistant to talking about certain subjects. In therapy I often notice that a person can talk about many things, then in a certain area, sometimes sexual but not always, she clams up and becomes resistant, even angry, if I press on with questions. It's like going to the dentist—you don't mind it too much if the dentist is touching your healthy teeth, but when he comes to a sore spot, ouch. So you respect the sensitivity of these sore spots. You don't go on cavalierly just because your own analogous tooth doesn't hurt. People have different sensitivities. You say outright that your partner does not have to talk about anything he doesn't want to talk about, that you will not pressure him. You may have similar sensitive areas, and you can mention these. I often talk about the fact that some subjects are too painful to talk about, focusing for a while on that fact, and eventually when rapport and confidence in my sensitive awareness build up, my patient starts talking about sensitive subjects without my asking. Be careful not to come across as condescending. You are not your lover's psychiatrist, and even if you were, you wouldn't want to be condescending. You are using an approach to open up communication, and in turn it can be used by your lover with you.

Sometimes people say they don't want to talk about something—they are perhaps frightened of their own emotion—and then they go ahead and talk about it anyway. For example, a patient entered my office who appeared distraught, grief-stricken. She handed me a note: "Dr. Harris, Today at 10:05 A.M., my dog died. She was my best friend. I don't want to talk about it. Okay?" I nodded, without saying a word, then she began to talk about it. When she handed me the note, I could have said, "What the hell are you coming to psychotherapy for if you don't want to talk about it? Don't you know we've *got* to talk about the important, painful issues in here? This is an insult to our psychotherapeutic relationship!" If I had done that, I would have been of no help to her.

If your ex-lover is especially resentful about your former sex life together, or lack of it, you will have to be extra sensitive when you bring up the subject of sex. Not because it shouldn't be discussed, but because your sudden interest in doing something about it may seem insincere, nothing more than a maneuver to get a lover back. If suddenly you can talk about it, why didn't you do so before? All that wasted time and frustration was truly unnecessary, it would seem. You could have done something *then,* but just didn't give a damn. Your answer to such complaints could be that *now* you realize your mistake, but in giving this answer, don't press the issue. Your ex-lover's anger deserves to be ventilated. If there was love present in your relationship, though she or he may have you logically cornered, your concern now, if persistent and not overdone, will have its effect after the anger plays itself out.

HOW TO TREAT YOUR EX-LOVER TO A SEXUAL SURPRISE

After Matt and Inge broke up, he sent her a note:

Sweetie,

If you return to me, I will love you with the quality of shared moments and the quantity and quality of physical passion that only unambivalent love can show.

—M.

"I see," she said aloud to herself. "The problem was he was ambivalent about me before. Now he's not."

She resented the note. She didn't believe a word of it, but she held on to it. For a long time she had wanted him to make love to her like that, but he had neglected her. She had attempted to please him in many ways. Occasionally he showed some interest, largely in *his* pleasure, but took her for granted, as though she didn't have sexual feelings. He acted as if women didn't need to be sexually pleasured. She was an attractive woman. Before meeting Matt, she had never doubted her womanliness. Then she came to feel insecure, used. When she met Zeke, what a release! She had forgotten how wonderful lovemaking could be. In the blush of her refound pleasure, there was no force on earth that was going to make her give that up and go back to Matt. Why should she trust Matt? She concluded, he had never really made love to her. And now this note! The arrogant jerk.

Fortunately for Matt, she had really loved him, and he had in his own halfhearted way had his moments when he loved her, though he had never communicated it very well, especially sexually. It was significant that she didn't simply crumple the note up and throw it away. Matt didn't know it. She wouldn't admit that to him, and she didn't owe it to him. It was not game playing. She was justifiably angry.

"Did you get my note?"

"Yes," she said with a bite of hardness to the word.

"Well?"

"Well, what? Do you expect me to say something to that bullcrap?"

"I want to make love to you."

Click. She hung up. Matt was crushed. How could she react to him that way? He felt as if he had made an obscene phone call. But then, he thought, how could he have taken her for granted for so long?

Matt managed to get dates with her. When he realized she wouldn't tolerate a physical come-on, he was hurt and furious, despite his better judgment, which told him she had a right to refuse him. What had always been available before was no longer available. He debated her on the subject. She won the debate. If he had loved her, how come he was interested only now? She had given him lots of time to recognize his "mistake," as he referred to it, but only now . . . He backed off, letting his better judgment take control. If the subject of sex came up from now on, he was ready to talk about it in a nondemanding way. If there was an opportunity to bring it up, he would. They continued to see each other. One night it happened—they made love. His approach was tentative and sensitive. She responded to that. He allowed himself to love her. He focused his attention on her body, not his need for her body, not even his need to please her, but on her pleasure. His own pleasure came of its own accord as she responded to him. Now she was really confused. The man she had always loved had discovered how to make love to her. His action, when he had a chance to express it, spoke more convincingly than his words. He was lucky to have the opportunity. He could never have demanded it.

If your ex-lover still makes love with you, then you have a great opportunity to surprise him or her with an unexpected increase in quality. If sex with your ex-lover is out of the question for now, then be ready when the opportunity arises. There is nothing quite as pleasantly surprising as a former lover who suddenly demonstrates a quantum leap in the art of love expressed physically.

If your ex-lover has discovered someone else who has cared enough to learn how to make love well, you're going to have to be patient. Good lovemaking triggers the limerance-bond I discussed earlier. All is not lost, though, because limerance and love are not the same thing, but you may have to let his or her sexual limerance play itself out. To try to force your ex-lover to give it up will lead to your frustration and to your ex-lover's resentment. You continue to love, but you do not force or demand. Look at it from the point of view of your goal. Your love, your presence may hurry your lover's return to you. Your anger and demands may increase the strength of your ex's limerance-bond with someone else.

But how are you going to become such a good lover all of a sudden? The more opportunities you have to practice with your lover, the better you will become, but the quantum leap occurs with an attitude change—a willingness to learn new ways of pleasing your lover, a willingness to learn an increased sensitivity to what is going on inside your lover's head. If you can do these things in the area of sex, it will become easier to love your lover in many other ways as well.

SO HOW DO YOU LEARN?

To begin with, you owe it to yourself, if you don't already know, to learn the basic techniques of lovemaking. You wouldn't hesitate to buy a book or videotape on racquetball or tennis or swimming if you were interested in those things. Why not for something as vitally important as sex? But sex is a mystery! Yes, it is and will always remain so, but the only thing that comes from a lack of talking, asking, reading, viewing, and finally trying is ignorance. Sex does not just happen. People who have successfully avoided any information about it until they're married literally don't know what to do first. Since this remains an age of relative sexual ignorance, even those who know the basic mechanics don't have the slightest wherewithal when it comes to passionate communication. You don't learn by spontaneous generation in the head. You learn by seeking out knowledge. Knowledge is presented better by some teachers than it is by others. Some teachers can make anything, even sex, offensive or boring. So seek out the good teachers.

You might start off by renting a copy of *Ryan's Daughter* from your local video store. Watch the whole movie if you like, but for the purpose of gaining a nodding acquaintance with intensely sensual, passionate sex, watch the forest love scene between the young soldier and the adulteress. Note that what is important is not just technique, it's the obvious physical communication that's taking place between the lovers.

If you don't have a VCR, consider some of the great romantic novels, such as *Lady Chatterley's Lover*, by D. H. Lawrence.

These are examples of the kind of communicating you want to learn how to do. Your lover will never forget what's being said. A word of caution—be patient with yourself. An analogy—if you're interested in communicating with music, and study how Beethoven did it (or Elvis Presley), you may figure you could never communicate that well, but be patient with yourself. You don't have to communicate that well, and if lovemaking becomes as important to you as music was to Beethoven or Elvis, you might.

Next I recommend that you rent or buy a copy of "Sexual Positions: A Modern Guide to Lovemaking," produced by MFM video (and praised, by the way, by the

Institute for Advanced Study of Human Sexuality), or another instructional tape. These tapes will teach (or review) the basics, and then some. The well-illustrated book *The Joy of Sex,* by Alex Comfort, M.D., should also be helpful.

You don't have to learn every technique there is to be a good lover. Some techniques you and/or your lover may even find offensive; then you know what to avoid. (Unless you start finding everything offensive, in which case you should consult a sex therapist.) Don't insist that your lover watch the film or read the books with you. Above all, learn to increase your sensitivity to your own body's feelings and do the same for your lover's.

WHAT ABOUT KINKY SEX?

Kinky can mean idiosyncratic, or peculiar to the individual, in which case, any sex that's good has to be at least a little bit kinky. There are the generalized techniques of good sex, sensitive touching, and kissing that vary from passionate to whispery, the standard positions of sex—books have been written about it—and then there's individualized lovemaking when you discover the right stroke, the right place, and the right timing that works for your lover, and that, simply because it's specific to the person, might be defined as kinky.

In sex you should never do what goes against the grain. On the other hand, if you love your lover, then you're going to be on the alert for the specialties that arouse your lover and you, or at least arouse your lover and are nonoffensive to you. Beware of passing judgments too quickly. Some things you just won't want to do, but attitudes can change, including yours. Some people, when they are rejected by their lovers, suddenly desire them back with an intensity and in ways they wouldn't have considered before—and they mean it, or may come to mean it, when they do it.

Alex and Sarah had a decent enough sex life, but nowhere near as exciting as she knew it could be. One day she finally told him a secret—it would really turn her on if during foreplay, he would talk "dirty." He loved her all right, and so he was willing to try, but though he went through the motions, he just couldn't put his heart into what he was saying, and his beloved remained unmoved. If she had wanted him to hurt her, he would have been right to refuse, but so long as it was harmless, well, she was making a reasonable request and should be encouraged to talk openly about any other requests she might have. If he loved her, he would experiment and try different things, and maybe one day he'd even give her the kind of excitement she'd like. Would that be perverted? Not to her.

Edna and Edward had a different kind of problem. One day during a therapy session Edna blurted out in great embarrassment that she had something to say. There were times when she caught her husband putting on her makeup! And sometimes her underwear! Once after they got home from a Mozart concert at a university, she discovered that he had been wearing her panties during the concert. She cursed him and called him a "homo." "He said that that's the way men dressed in Mozart's time! Why couldn't *he*? She exploded, she said, asking her husband, "Aren't you a *man*? I thought I married a *man*!" And, as she said to her therapist later, "If my husband is going to be a woman, what am I!?"

The therapist explained that he and his colleagues had worked with other couples for whom cross-dressing was an issue, and that cross-dressing, even if it continues, need not necessarily be a problem. Edna paused in her crying and studied the therapist. She was receptive, though cautious.

She and her husband had sex with each other regularly. They both enjoyed their lovemaking. No problem there. It's just that when she caught him doing those things he made *her* feel like a man. She began sobbing again.

Cross-dressing does not harm anyone. It also does not cause homosexuality. If the non-cross-dressing partner finds it offensive, then perhaps reassurance will be enough. It could be done when the offended partner is not around, but it should not be hidden; it's okay if one partner sees the other. It can be a secret the two lovers share but is not likely to be a successful secret that one lover hides from the other. Doing something forbidden and hiding it can add to the excitement. Edna's response to her husband was probably encouraging him to do it more.

If the cross-dressing bothers the person doing it, psychotherapy might help alter the behavior or decrease the feeling of being bothered by it. The best solution would be if this "kinkiness" could playfully be introduced as a part of this particular couple's bedroom repertoire, but that would require that both feel comfortable with their sexual identities. Reassurance is often enough in cases such as this, so long as sexual insecurity does not run deep.

Where do these kinky desires come from? That's not always clear. I suspect most often it is a matter of association. For example, men who reached puberty in World War II England often saw attractive young women with gas masks in the air raid shelters. They experienced their first really strong sexual urges at the time that they were looking, very naturally, at these sexy females with their gas masks. Years later, some of these men still feel sexually aroused by the sight of a gas mask. Is that really so bizarre? Perfume, lipstick, high heels also bring to mind women and the sexual arousal men associate with them. Some women are aroused by cigar smoke and tattoos. The list of possibilities is endless.

Wait a minute now, isn't anything that's kinky perverted? Something's got to be perverted, right?

Let's look at another example. A woman may enjoy stripping for a man. She enjoys the excitement in his eyes. The power of the physical response she elicits demonstrates her womanliness. She loves or at least likes her man or men, so she enjoys giving him the pleasure of visually caressing her body and she enjoys being visually caressed. She is communicating on a physical—visual—level. Some might consider it kinky, but it's all good and healthy.

What is good can be made "perverted." Take the case of a professional stripper who hates men and is stripping only to humiliate herself and gain power over men—that action is harmful and, I believe, perverse. Sex acts as excuses for uncaring power trips, hurtful sex, unloving sex—all these pervert the sex act into another realm of power and manipulation, not love.

GROUND RULES

You're going to get your lover back by loving 100 percent, and that means that if the opportunity for sexual expression arises, you're going to express affection, sensitivity, knowledge, and all the other good things that love does through sex. Take full advantage of any idiosyncratic pleasures your lover is prone to, so long as it is not physically harmful or painful to you or your lover. If you find a particular idiosyncrasy absolutely offensive, then admit it to yourself and, if the opportunity arises, to your lover, but find other variations that you are comfortable with. Remember also, and tell your lover, that you might change your attitude—something that's offensive now might not seem so at another time—this is a common event. If no variation is acceptable to you, then consultation with a sex therapist should be considered part of your preparation for getting your lover back.

If your lover is especially uptight about sex, then what a wonderful opportunity you have to love and guide him or her toward greater sexual fulfillment, so long as you proceed at a pace that is psychologically comfortable for your lover and you never insist or demand. Assisting your lover in his or her sexual liberation will create an incredibly positive memory of you within your lover's mind. But remember, all you can do is assist—the desire must come from your lover. To repeat a cliché, you cannot make someone want something.

If your ex-lover is so uptight about sex that even after you get him or her back, he cannot talk about it, cannot begin to consider any variation, then counseling—couple's therapy and then perhaps individualized therapy—is indicated. If there is love present on both sides of the love-bond, even if initially perhaps mostly on your side, this problem may be worked out. If there's something even more serious going on, then you will have to ask yourself if you're willing to accept the limitations of a love-bond with an impaired lover. (See chapter 10, "Loving Impaired Lovers, and Why People Bother.")

Do not use sex to manipulate nor allow yourself to be manipulated by sex. You do sexy things for your lover as an expression of love and/or because it feels good to you and vice versa, or you may trade sexual favors with your lover, but do not use sex nor allow sex to be used as a bargaining chip for things outside the sex act if your purpose is to create a love-bond.

Do not seduce your lover and then expect that seduction to mean that you automatically get him or her back. Your ex-lover will resent you for that and may be less likely to come back to you. And if your ex-lover happens to be among those who then believe that he or she owes it to you to come back, you are still no better off, for you are not getting a love-bond, you are getting someone tied to you out of guilt and false obligation.

If a man puts a hole in his condom to get "his" woman pregnant or the woman "tricks" the man into getting her pregnant, love is not in the picture, and the potential baby is the sad victim.

You owe it to yourself not to confuse sex with love, any more than you should confuse a shared hamburger or shared French cuisine with love, though these things are often associated with love. They can build the pleasant moments that are the foundation of love, but maybe they are just nice things that you share with someone, made more pleasant if that someone is a friend. People are not always in love when they experience the waxing of their sexual appetite.

Speaking of sexual appetite, one more thing to remember while we're discussing ground rules is that sexual appetites vary. The intensity and frequency of sexual desire varies from person to person. If you and your lover happen to be on the same sexual clock, then all the easier for you; but you may not be, and that's okay, so long as you recognize it and talk about it. That way nobody feels rejected or used. It's okay for one lover to pleasure the other and not be pleasured in return if there's no interest in being pleasured in return and if everything is voluntary on both sides. Sexual accommodation can be a part of love, but it's also okay simply to say "Later" or "Some other time" if you're not in the mood.

Finally keep sex in perspective. If sexual attraction is the primary force that is holding you to your former lover, then admit it to yourself. Don't grovel. Be considerate, and create pleasant moments whenever you get a chance, but don't confuse yourself or anyone else by calling sexual attraction love. And remember there *are* lots of sexy fish in the sea. It is not as important to save a particular relationship if sex is the bond, though there is nothing wrong with trying. If you develop a caring attitude toward the world and the people in it, develop confidence within yourself, and treat your own body as though you care about it, there's lots of sexy fish that are going to find you interesting, maybe even that particular sexy fish you've had on your mind so much of late.

YOUR BODY AS A GIFT

It is important not to get so caught up in the grief of being left by your lover that you mistreat your body. When Mary left Tom, for a while his appetite naturally dropped off; he was feeling kind of down and didn't care much about eating. He continued to exercise—it was an ingrained habit. He had not chosen to be on a diet. In this one instance his sorrow over being left by his lover benefited him; it actually improved the condition of his body. He lost his love handles. He became lean and muscular. Months later, when he had gotten his lover back, she remarked on how impressed she had been with his new body. It wasn't just that Mary found Tom attractive. The fact that his body was in shape meant that he still cared about himself and that therefore his caring for his lover was believable.

Genetic endowment gives some people an advantage when it comes to looks. There is no way around that fact, but there is variety to what attracts people. If you have been in a love-bond with someone, then your body is a variation that has worked for your lover.

People compensate for whatever failings their bodies may have with other qualities. In the maintenance of a love-bond, a degree of sexual attraction is nearly always essential, but more important is the ability to love and to communicate that love in a variety of ways.

Heredity can give some people an advantage, but the advantage is not absolute. It is what you do with what you have that communicates your basic attitude about yourself to the world. That attitude is the single most important factor in attracting other people to you. Without a good self-attitude, your hold on anyone in a love-bond is based either on deceit (you've managed to convince the outside world, though not yourself, that you think you're okay) or on pity (you're a charity case for someone with a soft heart), but neither of these holds will sustain a love-bond.

If you love yourself, doesn't it stand to reason that you'll take care of your body? The physical attraction that goes beyond endowment, the one that springs from the way you treat your body, through exercise, diet, hairstyle, and the way you dress and smell, is extremely important for two reasons: (a) It demonstrates that you care enough about yourself to make yourself attractive; and (b) It demonstrates that you care enough about your lover to make the sum total package "you" reasonably attractive—in fact, if you have the time, as attractive as you can.

Think about it. Would you give a slipshod, poorly wrapped gift to someone you care about? Think of your body as a gift to your lover. The care you take with your body is then a communication of your love.

WHAT SHAPE IS YOUR BODY IN?

Stand naked in front of a mirror. Look without flinching. If your ex-lover loved your body when it was anywhere near the shape it's in now, then anything you do to improve it is going to be a surprise bonus.

This is not an exercise or diet book, but a few words on these subjects in the spirit of our theme of total love of self so that you are able totally to love your ex back to you are in order. When a psychiatrist or psychologist hypnotizes a patient to help him diet or exercise, the hypnotism is merely an instrument to help the patient establish a new basic belief, a belief that is designed to alter the patient's self-attitude so that a change of behavior is possible. The hypnotism is sometimes a time-efficient means of establishing a new belief, but what is important is not the hypnotism, it's the belief. Ultimately our actions are determined by our beliefs in the same way that what a computer does is determined by the program you put into it. Without the right underlying basic belief, no diet book or exercise program is going to work.

In my psychiatric practice I have worked with many overweight (and underweight) patients. When a patient decides that he or she wishes to focus on getting her body in shape, the first step is to determine the patient's underlying beliefs. I have never met, for example, an overweight patient who was having trouble losing weight who did not have an underlying belief that was preventing weight loss. Many people are afraid of losing weight because they *believe* that if they did, they would not be able to resist the opportunity to cheat on their lover, or that they could not handle the new attention that they would get from the opposite sex, or that they could not handle the jealousy likely to be engendered in their current lover, or they're just *supposed to be* fat . . . and on the beliefs go. Sometimes out-of-shape bodies are expressions of anger. "Here, this is what you deserve!" one lover says metaphorically to another. "You deserve my overweight, out-of-shape body!"

Remember, our bodies are the way in which we communicate with the world. A woman got so angry over her father's ridicule of her mild weight problem that she deliberately gained over a hundred pounds. A lover could do that too. Poorly conditioned bodies can be an expression of depression or low self-esteem, or sometimes eating food seems to be the only way to pass the time or reward oneself. These beliefs ought to be unearthed and discarded the way you would discard a bad program that was messing up your computer.

How do you discard a negative belief? You recognize it for what it is. Every time you think it, you "unthink" it by telling yourself, "That's absurd." Most important you think out your new set of beliefs (write a new program) and keep suggesting it to yourself every chance you get. (See Shad Helmstetter's *What to Say When You Talk to Your Self.*) You could get a book on self-hypnosis or go to a hypnotherapist to use the technique of hypnotism to help establish your new belief.

A positive self-belief about your body would go something like this: Your body is your way of communicating with and living in the world. How well you communicate with and live in the world will in large part determine your happiness. You can make your body the best it can be by taking care of it. You owe it to yourself and those you care about to take care of your body. Consume good-tasting, nutritional food, the same way you'd use only quality gasoline for a quality car. You are quality. You need to exercise, the same way your car needs to be used from time to time, but you also need rest. The key is balance. Enough food, enough exercise, and enough rest. You deserve a balanced diet and a good balanced exercise program, and starting right now you're getting it. Any changes in your diet or exercise should be slow and progressive to give your body the time it needs to adapt to a new pattern, the kind of pattern you will be able to live with for a lifetime and enjoy.

Once you got these beliefs firmly into your brain, exercise and diet books might be able to help you. Maybe all you needed was an attitude toward your body that reflected self-love.

With your body in shape, you will be better able to express your love through physical-sexual communication. With a willingness to learn more about your own and your lover's sexual response, along with an insistence on mutual respect, your sexual loving will become an important component in your plan to love 100 percent.

Chapter 7
HOW TO GET
BACK IN TOUCH

Once you have a clear idea of the kind of relationship you had with your former lover, an understanding and control of your own emotions, and a knowledge of the approach to take when you are with your lover, you are ready to take the first big step toward reestablishing contact.

There are many ways of making initial contact. Remember, any contact that is not extorted from or forced upon a former lover is an opportunity to demonstrate the respect and love you have for yourself and for your former lover. In the discussion that follows the examples we will review the methods that are used and the circumstances that make those methods appropriate.

As you read through the following case histories—the first of a lover contacted after a breakup that resulted from the very common pattern of one lover taking another for granted, the second involving contacting a very bitter ex-lover—consider how the methods and circumstances apply to your situation. Note the following kinds of contacts:

- *Practical-necessity contact*—the contact that results because something needs to be taken care of, for example, dividing up the houseplants or removing your clothes from your ex-lover's apartment or vice versa
- *Accidental contact*—the contact that results from unplanned encounters, such as a meeting at the supermarket, or meeting as the result of continued pursuit of a shared interest, such as a health spa or exercise class
- *Casual dates*—an informal lunch to discuss things in general, or just to catch up
- *Mutually planned and agreed-upon shared time together*
- *A simple note* that communicates a casual good feeling or mutually pleasant thought
- *Cards* on holidays and special occasions
- *A carefully planned gift*

SAM AND STELLA: FINDING LOVE LOST THROUGH NEGLECT

Stella had argued with Sam about the idea, but he insisted that he did not want a monogamous relationship. He told her he felt free to date others if he wanted to, and it was okay if she did the same.

Sam was not only ambivalent, much of the time, he appeared indifferent to Stella. Every time Stella did go out with someone else, he was hurt and angry—but he didn't let Stella know. She, of course, was hurt and angry at his indifference. She had let him know how she felt, declared that she loved him and wanted to commit to only him. He turned a deaf ear to her, sometimes accusing her of pressuring him into more than he wanted. They did share wonderful times, but the intervals between those times were growing longer. She finally backed off, not wanting to pressure him. He remained indifferent. Her anger and hurt escalated. Their relationship of three years was about to come apart.

One night, Stella asked Sam if she could borrow his car. He looked at her, "Well, when do you think you'll be back?"

"By eleven."

"Okay," he said.

Later that evening Sam felt a nagging doubt. He had always been so sure of Stella. He knew it was crazy to live like this, feeling as strongly as he did about her.

It was nearing eleven, when he was overwhelmed with the premonition that he had lost her. He didn't know who she was with, but since the previous week, he had been ignoring the feeling that she was considering leaving him. It suddenly hit him with full force. *She's left me.* He tried to drive the thought from his mind, but he was scared. He made the commitment to himself that when she got back that night, starting from that point on, he'd really be more attentive to her. He couldn't finish his work. He didn't know where she was, had no way of contacting her.

After eleven he tried to go to sleep, but every fifteen minutes or so, he'd get up, go to the front of the house, and look out at the street. The sound of every car made him tense as he waited for it to turn into the drive, but then the car would pass.

At 5:30 A.M. she finally came home.

He exploded in anger. "Where have you been!? You were supposed to come back at eleven."

"I had planned to be here earlier. I'm sorry."

"What do you mean, you had *planned* to be here earlier?" He retreated to the issue of his car, though that was not the issue. With increasing anger, he blurted out, "You were using *my* car, you were supposed to bring *my* car home."

"Yes, I meant to," she said again calmly, "but I didn't.

I'm sorry. I have to get ready for work now." Her tone dismissed the relevance of the subject.

"What!? I've been up all night, pacing, waiting for you to pull in."

She looked at him for a fraction of a second as though he had just said something that *was* relevant, but then set up her mirror and began arranging her makeup. "I've got to hurry. I'm going to be late for work."

"I can't believe this. You take my car out all night, and this is all you say? You can't do this if you're going to be with me!"

"Pretty soon that won't be a problem."

"What?! Who is it?"

"None of your business."

"Tell me!"

"I'm going to be late for work." She was putting on her makeup, ignoring him.

He searched his mind for words. He couldn't focus his thoughts. Anger. He grabbed the mirror and flung it to the floor. She screamed, began to protest. He took the makeup and flung it across the room. "No!" she said, emotionally hurt and frightened.

Words came to his mind: "Tell me what's going on?! You can't do this to me!"

"Look, I've waited long enough for you," she said. "I'm not waiting anymore." She put on a sweater and went toward the door. She paused, "Now you've got me physically afraid of you."

"Don't hold that against me. I didn't touch you, and that's the only time I ever broke anything."

"I know," she said, staring at him. She turned to go.

He shouted after her, crying, "I love you!" (He hadn't said those words in many months.) He collapsed into a chair, sobbing.

"You don't know what love is," she said, with the finality

of judgment rendered in her voice. Outside, in the street, the sound of the bus, the one she always took. She slammed the door behind her as she left.

He called in to work sick, stayed at home all day, thought about what he might say when she called, but she didn't call. He had assumed . . . he cursed himself for not calling her at work. He had to get her back. He told himself that he had to convince her that he loved her.

WHAT CAN SAM DO?

Sam was in the process of losing Stella over several years. Their love-bond was already dissolving. Stella was the first to act decisively in response to what was happening. She had found a replacement for Sam, and perhaps that gave her the courage to walk away from something that, though it had seemed to have potential, was not working. It is because she took the decisive step that Sam finally experienced rejection. Stella had been experiencing rejection for some time. Immediately (and finally) Sam felt the loss and just as immediately determined that, really, he loved Stella all along and still loves her.

Let us assume that though his indifference made it weaker, there *was*, in fact, a love-bond. He's got that going for him. Sam now has two possible responses to his predicament.

The first option is that he could simply wait. Stella may return on her own. There's a chance that whoever she's involved with doesn't know how to love any more than Sam does. After all, true love is an art that many, perhaps most, people scarcely think about in any realistic fashion and rarely practice enough to get any good at it. Once the glow of newfound attention wanes, she may wonder what's going on with old Sam. Waiting, however, is definitely a risky proposition.

Stella may have honestly become convinced that Sam does not love her. She has waited a long time, grieved over the loss of their love-bond even while they were together, and has finally, truly given up. There's a strong possibility that when she didn't return that night, she had finally made her decision. She wasn't going to be hurt anymore. She wasn't going to waste her life waiting for Sam to make up his mind.

This takes us to Sam's second option. He must convince her that he still loves her. That's a tall order. He's got several years of increasing indifference to overcome. He is going to have to demonstrate in action that he does love her. However, because she left in response to his indifference, his first step to reestablish contact should be a decisive declaration of love. He's got to tell her somehow that he does love her. He has decided he loves her and is going to love her 100 percent to get her back and keep her. This means, for him, suppressing his need to protect his vulnerable heart and telling her what she needs to hear, a direct, concrete statement of love. She needs to know that information, even if, at first, she doesn't believe him, even if, at first, she is angry at him for telling her too late what she has wanted to hear. Once the information is communicated, he can continue to demonstrate his love by being understanding of *her* response.

If your lover left because you neglected your love-bond through indifference, the first contact should be a declaration of love. Please remember our discussions in parts I and II: This declaration should not become a declaration of your need. Your lover's need has gone neglected for so long that to hurtle your need at your ex-lover is to add insult to injury.

THE FLIP SIDE

The story of Sam and Stella does raise another question: Can an indifferent lover be won back? Could Stella have gotten Sam back without having to leave him?

Stella has not been indifferent. From her point of view she has been "loving" Sam all along but has been increasingly ignored. Sam even tells her to "date other guys." He has left her even though they are still together. How can she get him back?

Stella must find the answer to two questions: (a) Has she truly been *loving* Sam? Has she been accepting of his need for distance? It is possible that Stella has been focusing only on her own need for the reassurance of a commitment and thus, in her own way, ignoring Sam; (b) Or is Sam genuinely an impaired lover, incapable of loving Stella even in a pressure-free environment?

To answer these questions, Stella must first try to talk to Sam. "It's okay to be honest with me. I love you. Do you want to try to make this relationship work?" Sam may very well say he loves her but then avoid or rationalize why they don't do more things together. If Stella presses, complains, or insists that *he* suggest, on his own, how they might spend time together, he is very likely to sink farther into silence, spend more time with the boys or at work or in front of televised football games, more time with whatever his means of avoidance is. Stella can then love him with the amount of attention he enjoys but genuinely pursue her own interests. She can suggest an activity when she wants to do something together, but she ought not wait for him before she pursues her own interests. She must love herself and life too much for that.

If Sam loves her at all, it will be easier for him to recognize and demonstrate his love if it is also clear that Stella loves herself, independent of her relationship with him, and that her love for him is not contingent on his meeting her needs. Her self-love is demonstrated most clearly by her continued pursuit of other friendships and other interests.

If his attentiveness alternates with indifference, especially if the pattern is that as she spends more time with other interests, he gets nervous and focuses more attention on her and then if she returns his interest, he becomes indifferent (perhaps even complaining of being "suffocated" by the relationship), then he is showing signs of fear of intimacy.

If he does not work through this fear, he may be incapable of sustaining his end of the love-bond. If Stella discovers that *this* is the case, she can either leave Sam or read chapter 10 of this book, "Loving Impaired Lovers, and Why People Bother." She must come to terms with the reality of Sam.

Fortunately for Stella, Sam was confused, not impaired, and here's how he got her back.

SAM REESTABLISHES CONTACT

At 7:00 A.M., thirty-six hours after Stella walked out on him, Sam stood waiting for her at the large, open office area where she worked. Clerks and secretaries were having coffee and chatting, occasionally looking toward him. Some said "Hi." They recognized him as Stella's boyfriend. Perhaps some of them noticed that he looked distraught.

She did not notice him at first, but when she came in, he saw her instantly and walked toward her. She had turned to her left and was slowly walking away from him without knowing it. Her red sweater magnified her presence in his mind. He had not seen her for thirty-six hours. There she was, real as ever. She was saying "Hi" to someone, laughing with her friends. She seemed perfectly normal. How could that be?

A fellow worker said, "Oh, Stella, that's a beautiful sweater. Did he give it to you?"

"He?" she turned in the direction of the worker's glance. She saw Sam. He handed her a note. She glanced down at it, expressionless.

The note read:

> Stella,
>   I love you with all my heart.
>   Please come back to me.
>   —S.

This was the opening move in Sam's campaign to get his lover back, though he may not have thought of it that way at the time.

Stella could respond in any of three general ways. First, she might tell him to get lost or the equivalent. Sam's response to this could be that he means what he says but he doesn't want to make her feel uncomfortable, and then he could leave. The opening move still remains effective, even if her initial response seems to be total rejection. He has, believably or not, conveyed the information he needed to convey. His later actions will demonstrate whether or not he's telling the truth.

Second, Stella could remain polite, saying she doesn't want to hurt his feelings, they can remain friends, and so on. In response, Sam can say that he means what he says but he understands how she feels and he will respect her feelings. He would like to maintain contact with her. Whatever contact she agrees to can then be converted into opportunities to demonstrate his genuine love for her. This first encounter then becomes an excellent opening for him.

Third, Stella could, perhaps after a little hesitation, say that she loves him, too, and of course she will come back to him. This may very well be the worst of the three possibilities, especially since Sam and Stella have been in a troubled relationship for years. Habits of relationship style are hard to break. Without lots of extended communication and demonstrated loving, the love-bond is going to fall back to the old pattern. This response would indicate that Stella was not facing the fact that Sam was not yet trustworthy. Her lack of faith in herself away from Sam doesn't have much to do with a real love for Sam.

Whatever Stella's response, Sam is going to have to make a sustained effort to save their love-bond.

EARLY CONTACT BETWEEN THE NEW SAM AND HIS STELLA

Stella looked up from Sam's note. She asked, "Come back to what?"

"To us."

"Us?" She shook her head. "There's been no 'us' for a long time. Haven't you noticed?"

"Please! I can't stand another night. I go without sleep."

"I don't want to hurt you, but Sam, it wasn't working."

"I just want you to know that I love you. I know I wasn't making it very obvious, but I really do love you, and *if* . . . I realize it's only an if . . . but if I get another chance, I promise you'll know I love you."

"I'm involved with someone else now. I don't know, Sam. . . ."

"I don't blame you. Can we at least talk?"

It took several months, and Sam sometimes made mistakes, but he used *nearly* every opportunity he had—even when Stella was collecting the things she had left at his apartment—to demonstrate his understanding and sensitivity for her concerns.

Initially, they saw very little of each other. He sent her a dozen roses at work, just to let her know he still loved her, because whether or not he loved her was an issue for her. Then he sent a dozen roses a day for three more days. When she complained that it was "too much," he stopped sending the roses, despite his inclination to do otherwise, because he did not want to risk turning a gesture of affection into a gesture of manipulation or need.

He occasionally stopped by her workplace with a rose or an inexpensive gift. If by doing so, he had endangered her job, got the boss angry, or come to blows with a new boyfriend at work (again endangering her job), then he would hardly be demonstrating love. However, he found ways of making small gestures without causing conflict at work. For example, one of his pet names for Stella over their years together had been "Sugar." He arrived at her workplace early one day and left a box of sugar cubes with no card on her desk. She would know from whom it came. When Stella explained to her fellow workers the meaning of the gift, one of them said, "How cute!" Stella laughed along with them. A small, pleasant moment had been created. Over time such moments add up.

Familiar expressions, nicknames, fond memories, and endearing eccentricities can be gently called up to help get a lover back—that's one of the advantages of having already been in love with the very person you're courting.

It is unlikely to be the single incident or the single gesture that matters. It is consistency over time that counts. Each pleasant incident, every well-timed gesture, took Sam one step closer to his goal.

Being too predictable (showing up with the same gift every day) or too demanding (constantly and expectantly expressing your love) do *not* create pleasant feelings, though. Don't go overboard.

Sam and Stella began having lunch dates and then dinner dates, then a movie or a concert together. Sometimes they'd quietly read in each other's company. Eventually they were back in love, and in a much more viable relationship than the one they had had before the breakup. Who got who back depends on your point of view.

CONTACTING A RESISTANT LOVER

You may have driven your lover away through seriously irresponsible behavior. This happens. You are not alone. It may or may not be possible to make complete amends, but you can get your lover back in your life and work to heal the wounds.

Claudia is an alcohol abuser who neglected and verbally abused her husband and children every time she went on a binge. When she'd sober up, she'd put her life together for a while, apologize, profess her love for her husband and children, promise never to drink again, but then she'd drink again, until the repeating scenario got so predictable that neither she nor anyone else believed her promises. This negative pattern had established itself over many years. Finally her husband came home one day to find her passed out drunk on the living room floor and the children roaming the house naked, hungry, and looking for food. He decided that enough was enough and took the children and left.

When I saw Claudia in therapy, she said she'd just as soon be dead. In addition to her depression, she was also very angry about the seeming finality of her husband's rejection of her. She had to admit, however, that if her husband would agree to take her back, he'd be pretty dumb. There was no reason to believe that she wouldn't binge again.

Time passed. She progressed in therapy and became a dedicated member of AA. She recognized her own progress. Paradoxically her progress frustrated her, because her husband still would have nothing to do with her.

I pointed out to her that she should be proud of her husband—he was pretty smart. It was going to take time to convince him that she had really changed, just as it had taken time to drive him and her family away. Her in-laws and husband were furious with her and very protective of the children.

In this type of situation the only solutions are to go very slowly, be very patient, and always consider the needs of those you love.

I suggested she use every opportunity to send a card— no great declaration of love needed. Birthday cards, Halloween, any excuse, gentle but caring, eventually the message would get through. For months there was no response to her cards. Finally there were phone calls . . . and then she began to see her children and meet with her husband. She took each opportunity to demonstrate her caring despite the rejection—something that can be done only without making demands. She and her spouse have not yet decided to get back together, and they may not, but there is no more rejection involved. They still see each other, talk with each other, and discuss ways of being better parents to their children. Claudia has what she wants.

Usually, even in the seemingly worst-case scenario, when an ex-lover refuses all contact, there are eventually still opportunities for contact. The mistake would be to respond to initial rejection by trying to force yourself on your ex-lover, for to do so will only increase resistance. No matter how adamantly your ex-lover insists that he or she does not want to see you, time may change attitudes. In fact, there could even be a reversal of roles, so that you become the pursued. If you attempt to force yourself on someone, you destroy the potential healing power of time. Imagine, in the above example, the negative effect that would have resulted had Claudia *insisted* early on that her family spend time with her.

Opportunities for contact will vary, but they will nearly always arise. Perhaps an article of clothing needs to be picked up, or a card could be sent on a birthday or some other occasion. Most attempts at getting a lover back fail not because of a lack of opportunities for contact but because those opportunities that do occur are not taken proper advantage of.

Gently let it be known that you are there. Send a card on birthdays and holidays. Keep your comments simple. If your ex-lover already knows that you love him, then it is not necessary to beat him over the head with the fact. It may be better simply to sign your name with no special comment other than "Happy Birthday" or "Merry Christmas," and so on. Remember, you are doing this to get your lover back, not to experience the pleasure of expressing your feelings.

If you have been in any kind of serious, love-based relationship, even after a breakup, your letters are going to be read. If the breakup was especially hostile, then you may at first get a "Return to Sender" response, but after a cooling-down period, usually you are going to be read, and often you'll be read even before a cooling-down period takes place. (Make sure *you* are cooled down before reestablishing contact.)

If your letter is being intercepted by a meddling relative,

acquaintance, or new "friend" of your ex-lover, try different routes of delivery.

Letters can sometimes bridge gaps that direct contact
would not. They are a way of saying what you have to say
without imposing the pressure of the response that would
be required if you were standing there. What should your
letter contain? The generic answer to that question is
whatever is the most considerate expression of love for
your ex-lover. Some people like to be told in purple detail
how much they are loved, others respond better to understatement. If they are based on your assessment of the
situation, statements of love would be experienced as a
burden, so keep the letter light.

Consider the following example:

> Dear Bob,
>   I love you with a love that runs deep. The kind
> of love that builds homes. And creates children. I
> myself did not know until shocked with the possibility
> of love's loss just how deeply I love you. Your feelings,
> your happiness, your clarity of mind mean everything
> to me. Even if I must wait until you want to be with
> me again, I will wait.

That letter might be the beginning of something new (it
was, by the way). On the other hand, if Bob were already
feeling trapped, the loving thing to do would be to confine
the above note to a shoe box.

Use your knowledge of your ex-lover and the particulars
of your situation to be innovative.

Linda was confused about her feelings. She had sepa-
rated from her husband but did not know if divorce was
the next step to take. Her husband, in a panic, started
loving her the way he did when they first met, only he was

"coming on like gangbusters," to use her expression. His words confused her. She told him to back off, not to call her, write to her, or anything. "No more words!" she declared. "I've got to sort out my feelings."

He sent her a three-page letter with no words. On the first page was a large exclamation point, on the second page a question mark, and on the third page a sketch of three tear drops. They laughed about that letter when they got back together.

GIFT GIVING AND OTHER ROMANTIC GESTURES

A professor of mathematical physics stopped by a bakery every morning on the way to the university. His small early-morning class of advanced students appreciated the treat he brought them. Little was said of it other than "Thanks," but the gesture strengthened the teacher-student bond. The teacher's patience with what were to him obvious mistakes as his students worked their way, at varying rates, through the intricacies of higher math, along with mutual understanding and joint effort, had created the teacher-student bond, which in the truest sense of the word was a kind of love-bond. Hot doughnuts every morning, even if the students hadn't always eaten them, gave the bond warmth.

The romantic gesture has this in common with mathematics: It is a shorthand language that says with precision what words would perhaps more awkwardly and cumbersomely express.

One of the rewards of going to the bakery every morning was the regular encounter with the lovely woman who sold the pastries. The logistics of picking what kind to buy, asking her opinion, sampling, and then talking while he counted out the money established an easy rapport between the professor and the young woman, but the professor was a little awkward with words. One day he brought her a single yellow rose, and the relationship took an instant leap forward. Shared experience, a gesture, and then her smiling response to the gesture, despite his awkwardness with everyday words, established the beginnings of a romantic relationship.

Possible gestures are myriad. There is the grandiose, overwhelming gesture, which, unless well-timed and appropriate to the context, is likely to seem manipulative, and then there are more subtle gestures that make understatements with impact.

Though a grandiose gesture can have powerful impact, if it misfires, it is more likely than the subtle gesture to delay getting a lover back. It is not just that it may seem manipulative, it also may demean the giver, because it can be seen as evidence of the giver's lack of faith in herself. Even if the grandiose gesture succeeds, its success may have been the success of manipulation, not of love, and if you are ever down on your luck and can no longer afford the grandiose gesture, then your relationship will dissolve just at the time when you feel the most need. Even if you are never down on your luck, you will never experience the healthy sense of well-being that comes from a relationship based on love. That is the risk of the grandiose gesture.

THE USUAL QUALITIES OF THE RIGHT GIFT

• *Unexpected.* Birthdays are important, but, to borrow an idea I remember from *Alice in Wonderland*, "Happy Unbirthdays" provide more opportunities, and can be more significant. Sad to say, established holidays lose some of their specialness by the very fact that they are established. We are expected to give gifts on Christmas, and so forth. On the other hand, established holidays do provide an opportunity to give a gift to an ex-lover that will be inherently an understatement, because it is expected. In the touchy situation where an ex-lover does not want anything at all to do with you, a Christmas gift might get through. Established holidays should always be remembered, especially if they are particularly important to your ex-lover. A forgotten birthday is grounds for divorce in some relationships. But don't forget to celebrate former President James K. Polk's birthday, by giving a gift to the one you love.

• *Nonmanipulative.* Gifts—to get your lover back—should express affection and, therefore, should be freely given without expectation of payment in any form. Do not, for example, trick your lover into accepting an expensive gift and then attempt to use that gift to inflict guilt.

"I just gave you a pair of five-thousand-dollar earrings, and you're still going to see that bastard?!"

She ought to throw the earrings at him and walk away.

• *Specific.* Don't just buy or make "a gift," buy or make *the* gift that is specific to your ex-lover. This is where knowledge of your ex comes in. A gift that is particularly appropriate for your particular ex-lover demonstrates awareness and sensitivity.

Remember, for example, Sarah's gift of fossil trilobites for Charles in *The French Lieutenant's Woman*? It was her initial gift. It demonstrated that she had observed him with enough care to know what his interests were. Had he been into ice-skating instead of trilobites, she might have given him a tiny sculpture of ice skates instead.

• *Inexpensive.* Expense is no proof of love. The more expensive the gift, the more specific it ought to be to the person and/or to the occasion.

If, for example, the real issue at hand is marriage, then an expensive diamond ring, so long as it doesn't bankrupt you, might be appropriate, but usually not as a gift to reestablish contact after a serious breakup. You might give a five-cent plastic ring with the statement, "This is just an experiment to check out the size." As an initial gift—to reestablish contact—this is okay only if the real issue is marriage and if your ex-lover has a sense of humor.

• *More than once.* Gifts ought to be part of the pattern of a romantic relationship. A gift to make contact that succeeds starts to seem manipulative after the fact if, after success, there are no more gifts.

Gifts are an important kind of communication that cannot be substituted for, any more than words can substitute for music or pictures. All avenues of communication are important in a love-bond, and gift giving is a kind of communication. One gift is never enough, but the timing and nature of the giving should vary, so that the giving does not lose its effectiveness by becoming expected.

CARING GESTURES

Sir Walter Raleigh threw his cloak over a puddle of water so that Queen Elizabeth would not get her feet wet. You need not drench your cloak (or coat), but you might walk with your ex-lover around the puddle, being ever alert to the opportunity to demonstrate caring. In *Annie Hall* Woody Allen goes over to his ex-girlfriend's apartment in the middle of the night, at her request, to kill a spider. That's a caring gesture. (Unfortunately Woody Allen is too caught up in the injustices inflicted upon him to love her back to him effectively—but it is funny and educational to watch him try.)

Michelle and her ex-boyfriend, Tom, used to drive through New England in the autumn looking for covered bridges. One day after their breakup, Michelle left one of her amateur paintings of a covered bridge on the front seat of her ex's car—there's a couple in the picture that looks suspiciously like Michelle and Tom, though no one can be sure.

Part of caring is self-restraint. You may, for example, offer your ex-lover a ride home but ought to allow him to refuse if he'd rather get home some other way. You are trying to do something for him by taking him home. You do not want him to do you a favor by allowing you to take him home. If he wants to walk in the rain or buy his own groceries, then let him.

An honest declaration of love that does not force the issue, a simple request to spend time together, matter-of-fact shared time to sort out business, chance encounters, thoughtful notes and letters, romantic and caring gestures—any or all of these can, depending on your circumstances, be used to reestablish and maintain contact. *Any communication that touches your ex-lover without applying pressure brings you one step closer to getting your lover back.*

Chapter 8
CREATING PLEASANT MOMENTS

Remember the pleasant moments, the times of real connection shared between you and your ex-lover? Moments like those helped bring you and your lover together. Those moments and the memories of them were the major reasons that you and your lover remained together as long as you did. By creating more of them you can strengthen or even re-create a love-bond. Opportunities to create these moments will vary, depending on the specifics of your situation, but it is important to take maximum advantage of *any* opportunity that presents itself or that you are able to create. And that includes opportunities that occur in what seem to be negative circumstances.

You cannot argue your lover back to you. Getting your lover back has little or nothing to do with winning arguments. It has everything to do with the mutual experience of pleasant or positive moments. Such moments consist of two things: you and the surrounding environment. Sometimes you can affect your surrounding environment, but always you can control yourself—the way in which you handle your environmental circumstance.

Once when on a date with Ana, John was turning his car around by backing it into a steeply curved driveway, which partially tore the muffler off the bottom of his car. He had to crawl under the car and bend the muffler back into place to prevent its scraping the road. Still the racket was awful. But he did not let the predicament get to him. He remained good-natured and calm and did not lose his temper. No sense making it worse. His date was impressed with his calmness in the face of adversity. Though the circumstance was unpleasant, Ana still enjoyed John's company.

One time when on a date with my ex-lover, trying to get her back, I took her to see the movie *Fantasia,* which neither of us had ever seen before. We both thoroughly enjoyed it, talked extensively about it afterward, laughing together at the amusing moments of the movie, which were now a common experience. Going to movies with a lover is, as most people are aware, still a great way to build a bond with someone. It's a significant kind of shared experience and should not be taken lightly just because it's so easy. When the movie ended, I had to take her back to her apartment. I knew she would be seeing someone else the next day. I was struck by the realization that the next night I'd be without her and she'd be with someone else. I felt a sudden sadness and the impulse to protest when dropping her off. But I held back, reminding myself that it had been a pleasant evening for both of us. I knew that an unusual movie like *Fantasia* would replay its scenes in our minds, and when it did, we'd remember who we were with. Why should I ruin the evening with an outbreak of protest? She already knew I loved her and wanted her back. I managed to suppress my impulse and left without soiling our good time with my needy feelings.

In the movie *Brainstorm* (1983 version) Michael Brace, Ph.D., leans over the railing of a stylish wood porch and shouts at his son in the pool below, "Chris, Chris, I told you to get out of the pool," then protests to his wife, "He pays no attention to me."

His wife, Karen, whom he's divorcing, speaks calmly, a tone of unrushed, unaffected understanding in her voice, "I'll get him, Mike . . . Chris."

Chris is swimming the breaststroke a few feet below them. He seems oblivious to his parents.

"Hurry up," says Mike.

"Chris," calls Karen. She reaches out with her foot to tap Chris's head as he goes by. He starts to climb from the pool.

The real estate agent enters in the company of the young buyers of Mike and Karen's house. "Doctor Brace." She repeats his name to gain his attention. "Doctor Brace, I'd like to introduce you to Doctor Harris."

The stranger steps forward. "Call me Ted."

"Ted," Mike acknowledges the stranger.

"Janet," says the woman stranger, identifying herself as she comes up from behind the man.

"You saw the house before?" asks Mike, faint recognition in his voice.

"Yeah, yeah. We're sold. Just want to get all the details."

"We signed all the papers today," Janet says.

"Good," Mike says. His son is on the porch. He hands him a snorkel. "That's for you."

"All right," says his son. "You got the right one," as if pronouncing a verdict, as he grabs it. He walks off quickly.

His mother says softly to him, "Say thank you." The calm, understanding tone does not leave her voice.

Mike is speaking to the buyers. His words, matter-of-fact on the surface, carry the faint note of sad emotion. "As you can see, this is a very special house, spent a lot of time to get it right." Breaking off, perhaps a little irritated by his feelings, he says to the real estate agent, "Why don't you show them the house?"

Janet says in a tone that is too superficial to be truly appreciative, "The house is wonderful. Ted likes all the special things you've done." (Doesn't she see it herself? Can either one of them possibly see what really went into that house, the caring that went along with the work and thoughtfulness? The home as a metaphor of what two people felt and hoped?)

The strangers are led off by the real estate agent.

Mike asks Karen, "Do you like them?"

"No." But she adds, focusing on the reality that is blurred by sadness, "It's theirs now."

"I know. I can't stay here now."

"Oh, well, that's okay," says Karen. "I can, ah, take care of all the packing and stuff."

"Sure?"

"Sure."

"It's a lot to do," he reminds her. "You have cardboard boxes?"

"Yes." She smiles, and laughs slightly. "I have cardboard boxes. I can take care of it all. Don't, don't worry." (You can hear her love for him in the tone of her voice.) She adds, "You could go live over at the Center." (That is, the research center where he works). "Lillian's there" (a fellow researcher and friend—not a rival in romance).

"Mmmm. Hmmm." A noncommittal expression on his face.

Mike is divorcing Karen. As we find out later in the movie, he has felt "suffocated" by her. In this scene, however, there is no suffocation involved. Mike is focused on the loss of the house. Karen is focused on loving him. She understands what he is going through and attempts to lessen his sadness. She offers to take care of getting everything out. Karen's understanding response to his emotion makes the moment more tolerable. He is experiencing being loved.

Notice also how Karen attempts to buffer the effect of Chris's rebuke of his father. Chris is ignoring his father, and when given the snorkel as a gift is almost rude in his acceptance of it. Karen intervenes persistently, but without getting angry, to get Chris out of the pool. Her concern for Mike is again expressed when she attempts to elicit a "thank you" from Chris. Karen, though firm with Chris, is not angry with him. She understands that the divorce is difficult on Chris as well. Karen is the loving person in this scene. She is touched by Mike's lingering sadness, who is reluctantly letting go. It is obvious that there had been a real love-bond between Mike and Karen and that love is still present. Chris, a child, is caught up by his hurt; his parents, unlike most divorcing couples, are not. Karen's love cannot transform the sadness of the moment, but it has transformed their mutual experience into a positive one. With more such moments the divorce would (and eventually does) become unnecessary.

How different is this scene from the usual embittered feuding between ex-lovers in a divorce! The court battles, the fighting over possessions, arguments about custody, attempts to enlist children and mutual friends as allies in a divorce war, create an endless number of bitter, negative experiences, so that a former lover comes to represent all that is bad and reconciliation becomes impossible.

SUPERCHARGED MEMORIES

Brainstorm centers around the invention of a remarkable device, a lightweight headset that records all of the wearer's sensory experiences. Whoever wears the headset when it's played back can experience what has been recorded *totally*—smell, sound, sight, taste, touch, and emotion. Besides entertainment and educational value, the device has applications for enhancing interpersonal understanding. You could literally experience what it is like to be me by playing one of my tapes, and I could experience what it is like to be you by playing one of your tapes.

Mike is one of the inventors of the Brainstorm device. Karen has designed the miniaturized headset version, so that a user need not wear bulky headgear. In another scene from the movie, her version is about to be tested. Karen enters.

She says, showing Mike the headset, "Hot off the mold. Take a look." (She obviously wants to please him, and would like a little attention.)

"Looks great," he replies matter-of-factly. He turns away to check something, perhaps an instrument panel or monitor. "Sit. Please."

She echoes his words with irony as she sits, "Looks great. Sit. Please."

He says, "Empty your head."

"Empty my head?" She studies him, soft irony in her words and expression.

He remains oblivious as he readies the equipment, then, saying "Okay," places the Brainstorm device on her head for a test run of the miniaturized version. "Just relax."

"Empty my head and relax."

A transitory expression on his face indicates that he may have finally noticed the irony in her words, but he continues the test.

Lillian intervenes, smiling. "Just lean back and forget everything. It'll be okay." Karen complies.

"That's good," he nods, and takes the device off her head. He places it on his own head. He pushes Playback.

Suddenly, he sees himself through her eyes. Her memory has been recorded, and he is experiencing it. He sees himself as she approached him just a moment ago. "Hot off the mold," she is saying, holding out the headset toward him. (Remember, he is feeling what she felt too.) Then there is a flashback to one of her earlier memories. He sees himself shouting at her, "You can take the house! the kids! the car!, the whole goddamned thing. I don't want anything! I'll live in a hotel. What about my work? I can't live like this, Karen!"

Mike, while seeing himself through her eyes, also feels her anger and remembers his own anger. Distracted and appearing a little insane in the context of the laboratory, he says to himself, as if he were Karen, "Go. Why don't you just go?"

Lillian intervenes, turning off the Brainstorm device. She asks Karen, "What were you thinking?"

"You mean, when you were recording my thoughts? I was thinking about my, ah, new design." She smiles, a soft sad sound in her voice. "But he always ignores me, and it just made me furious."

Lillian smiles. "Feelings." Her smile is on target. Significant communication has taken place.

Karen smiles.

Successful lovers create positive moments by retaining awareness of each other's point of view. Really successful lovers are able to imagine themselves inside the other person. This is called empathy, and the ability to empathize is a powerful skill in human relationships. It goes far beyond sympathy, which is a more superficial recognition of someone else's experience, though even sympathy goes beyond the indifference of being immersed to the point of oblivion in one's own feeling state. Caution is in order— until the Brainstorm device is invented, you can't assume you are correct in how you imagine it is to be someone else; you must validate your suppositions by asking and observing.

Because of Karen's knowledge and observation of Mike, she successfully loved him even when they were in the process of moving out of their common home. In the scene in the laboratory when Mike suddenly becomes aware of Karen's feelings, initially he is angry at both of them. Since real communication is taking place, the anger is not the damaging kind. Despite the fury, the incident in the laboratory has been another positive moment.

Mike uses the Brainstorm device to splice together a whole series of memories. He sees himself again and again from Karen's point of view, both the good and the bad. In the process he comes to understand Karen and reestablishes contact with his love for her. He then takes his tape and plays it for her. She laughs as she reexperiences happy moments with him, understands better the difficult moments, and reexperiences the feeling of awe that comes from the recognition of a bond created out of mutual love. More than ever—as a result of an accumulation of shared moments, the memory of them and the new, loving empathy—they love each other. The important thing is that even what seem to be negative moments become positive, love-bond-building ones when handled properly, and they add up with the happy moments, the cumulative impact being greater than the sum total.

THE FORMULA FOR GETTING A LOVER BACK

Each moment you share with your lover is important. What you do with any particular moment counts. Cursing, name-calling, pouting, begging, accusing, and demanding are not going to get your lover back. Communication based first on your awareness that your lover has a point of view and then empathy with that point of view *will* get your lover back, because that kind of communication creates positive, even happy moments, renders negative moments happy, elicits positive memories and, as we have seen in our example from *Brainstorm,* can change negative memories into positive new understandings.

If you're so inclined, you might think of your campaign to get your lover back in terms of a mathematical formula. If p = a positive moment, n = a negative moment, and i = the intensity of a moment, then the greater the p times i's in your love life, and the less the n times i's, the stronger your love-bond. $p \times i > n \times i = love$

HOW YOU GET GOOD AT CREATING POSITIVE MOMENTS

Some people just can't seem to help themselves. If the muffler falls off the car, they get out-of-control angry and take it out on everyone around them. This becomes a pattern, so that whenever anything goes wrong, they become inconsiderate of those around them, and therefore, because any relationship has its moments when things go wrong, they become less capable of sustaining a relationship. If they want things to go better, they're going to have to learn to care what happens to others, even during moments of discomfort.

In chapter 6 I discussed the importance of a caring attitude toward the world. We become good at caring and then at creating positive moments by practicing with friends, acquaintances, and even ourselves alone every chance we get. We can learn to be aware of our own feelings; we can learn to care for ourselves even during moments of adversity, and then we can learn to do the same for others by extension. The ability to relate successfully to others is a skill. One of the most demanding uses of that skill is successful loving within the context of a romantic relationship.

In *The Art of Loving*, Erich Fromm makes a useful analogy. If you wanted to be a great painter, you wouldn't wait until you stumbled upon a fantastic scene that seemed to call to you to paint it, because in that case, you would lack the skill to do so when the moment occurred. You would learn your art through reading, discussion, and most important, through practice. Just as it is with the art of painting, so it is with the art of loving. If you wait only for those moments when you're with your one true love to practice loving (which requires so many things—knowledge, empathy, awareness of one's own feelings, and so on), then you are not going to be ready to love.

You get good at creating positive moments by practicing the skill of doing so at all times. Then you make doubly certain you practice it every encounter you have with your ex-lover, accidental, planned, over the phone, or through the mail—even when, especially when, things are not going your way.

THE SETTING AND ROMANCE

In romance the setting can do more than half the work. Music, lighting, flowers, perfumes, colognes, a beautiful backdrop—mountains or sea, for example—can induce, just like induction into a trance, a romantic frame of mind. This is not surprising. A romantic frame of mind is a special kind of trance. A trance is essentially an intense focus on something, so intense that everything extraneous to it is blocked out. In a hypnotic trance the hypnotist asks the subject to focus on something, say a watch or a point of light, and to focus on that alone with all available concentration. Then the hypnotist can begin to make other suggestions. In romance a couple cooperates in trance induction, though they may not be aware of it. For example, candles in a poorly lit room attract the eyes as if mesmerizing them, as can the face of the right lover seen through the flickering light. Some people are more affected by setting than others, and some of settings are more powerful than others.

The setting or environment conditions us in many and often subtle ways, both romantically and otherwise. Habitual drunkards begin to slur their speech, talk loosely and even alter their gait upon entering a bar before a single drop of alcohol passes their lips, for the familiar environment of the bar itself suggests behavior and a frame of mind. Moviegoers slip into a trance state at the start of a movie, forgetting that they are in a seat inside a crowded theater, even forgetting with whom they are sitting—it is as if the spirit leaves the body and enters the movie. Thoughts, heart rate, breathing rate, even the flow of saliva, and peripheral body temperature respond to the images projected on the screen and to the accompanying sounds. The person who watches movies and says that he cannot be hypnotized does not know what he is talking about. Even the associated rituals of buying the tickets, entering the carpeted theater, taking in the aroma of popcorn, and so on, help induce a trance state, and so it is with romance too. The elements of the environment that induce a romantic trance can be either obvious or subtle— in Harlequin Romances we see the obvious, in Shakespearean plays we see both.

A pleasant, beautiful setting can be a powerful instrument in the hands of a determined lover. The ease with which you can find or arrange settings will to some extent depend on where you live. Living in Hawaii, or at the foot of the Alps, or in Venice, for example, has its advantages, but even Kansas has its breathtaking fields of wheat. Even if some poor lover lives in a flat, treeless, waterless terrain in the middle of a huge trailer park, a small candlelit paradise can be created inside a trailer.

You want to create a romantic trance state that will open up your ex-lover's heart to you once again. There are well-known settings that tend to elicit a romantic trance state, but to some extent, tastes differ. A knowledge of your ex-lover's tastes goes a long way. Setting includes *lighting*. Sunlight coming through a canopy of leaves can be just as effective as light passing through stained-glass windows in producing a receptive frame of mind. There is also candle-light, moonlight, starlight, and the lightning of a distant thunderstorm. (Some sources of light—and other special effects—are easier to plan for than others.) You can try soft light in a darkened room or shadowy light or light that enhances the scenery—and, remember, you are part of the scenery.

Setting includes *music*. Music physically affects the human brain. The rhythm of music literally affects the brain's bioelectrical rhythm. No wonder it plays a role in movies of all kinds, reflecting and accentuating every emotion portrayed, including the emotion we associate with romantic moments. The type of music depends on your ex-lover and you. Jazz can be soft and romantic, and so can classical music. Music, at least during part of your time together, should be low enough in volume to allow for conversation.

Setting includes *scents*—flowers, colognes, perfumes, and you. Even macho-type men, although they may be reluctant to admit it, are very much affected by the flowery scents and style of clothing of the women they love.

Setting includes *background*—a gondolier on a Venetian canal, beautiful paintings, a well-mannered waiter, other couples in a romantic setting, and so on.

Automatically, if you are in tune with the setting and allow yourself to relax, your gestures and the tone of your voice will become part of the setting. Ideally the two of you should be alone, or apart from the others around you.

These are the basic ingredients of setting. The main thing to remember is to keep it pleasantly comfortable and relaxed. You cannot force someone to share a pleasant moment with you. You can invite, to some extent you can plan, but you have to make the best of what you have—the time your ex-lover shares with you and whatever is available in your surroundings—if not a warm midsummer's breeze, then maybe a heavy snowfall, or a hot night with cold beer and pizza in a trailer park. You can take advantage of the setting to suit your situation.

Remember, the relaxing hypnotic effects of a setting will get your lover back only if your actions are always based upon the underlying principle of loving 100 percent. The result of acting according to that principle is the creation of pleasant, constructive moments. If it is possible to arrange an event, then you can use the setting to intensify a pleasant moment, as being careful not to overdo it. Candles, music, and obvious signals of your romantic intention are appropriate only if the timing is right, which means *when* your partner as well as you will enjoy them. It is also important to remember that attitude comes into play even in unpleasant situations, as we saw in the example from *Brainstorm,* when Karen created a positive moment out of the sad situation of a couple selling a home after a breakup.

There are times when not just the situation but your ex-lover himself can make the creation of a positive moment especially difficult. So, in part IV, we will look at how to handle things if the harsh reality of a resistant lover interferes with your attempts to work the magic of loving 100 percent.

PART IV

Love in the Real World

"Naught's had, all's spent
Where our desire is got without content."
—William Shakespeare, *Macbeth*

Chapter 9

DEALING WITH A RESISTANT LOVER

As much as you may try to make every contact positive and to create pleasant moments, your ex may fight your efforts. At times it may seem as if your ex is determined to create a negative moment. Also, after your initial contact, old problems and arguments will return, and you must be better prepared to deal with them unless you want to repeat the same negative patterns that led to your breakup. In this chapter we will look at how to apply your guiding principle—loving 100 percent—to these difficult problems.

AN ANGRY AND ARGUMENTATIVE EX-LOVER

If your ex-lover seems to want to criticize you or fight with you every time you come into contact, think before you respond in kind. Your ex loved you once, then something about your actions compelled him to leave. He may still have angry feelings he needs to express. To test you— after all, this attentive you is new to him; he'd rather test you now than trust you blindly and have to go through the pain of leaving you again—he may appear to take advantage of your 100 percent loving responses by using your openness to tell you what's wrong with you. To make it through this time, remember, unless your lover is impaired (see chapter 10), this testing stage will pass, as long as you remain as calm as possible and *always* remember your purpose: Is it to win an argument? To score points in a verbal dueling match? To crush your lover's ego? Or is it to convince your lover you love him?

In his autobiography, Benjamin Franklin wrote,

> When another asserted something, that I thought an Error, I deny'd my self the Pleasure of contradicting him abruptly, and of showing immediately some Absurdity in his Proposition; and in answering I began by observing that in certain Cases or Circumstances his Opinion would be right, but that in the present case there appear'd or seem'd to me some Difference, &c. I soon found the Advantage of this Change in my Manners. The Conversations I engaged in went more pleasantly. The modest way in which I propos'd my Opinions, procur'd them a readier Reception and less Contradiction; I had less Mortification when I was found to be in the wrong, and I more easily prevail'd with others to give up their Mistakes and join with me when I happen'd to be in the right. And this Mode, which I at first put on, with some violence to natural Inclination, became at length so easy and so habitual to me, that perhaps for these Fifty Years past no one has ever heard a dogmatical Expression escape me.

When my lover left me, one of the first things I did was to arrange for a meeting in a restaurant "to talk." I was going to argue her into believing that she was wrong to leave me and ought to come back immediately. As the argument proceeded, I finally realized that *I* was wrong on some major points—one of the biggest being that I had given such high priority to my career that I had left almost no time at all for a meaningful relationship, certainly not enough time for building a love-bond. She told me there was nothing wrong with giving total priority to a career but that I ought to be honest enough to admit that I didn't have time for a relationship and be done with it. When I said, "Well, this is just for now; things will get better," she reminded me that I had been saying that for years, and life does not last forever. Even the parts of my argument where I perhaps was correct (such as the time I had to neglect everything to study for a major licensing exam) didn't matter. The sum-total effect of my neglecting to love was too overwhelming. My winning those points in the argument was not going to soothe my ex-lover's anger. She was going to come back to me only if she decided, independently of the pros and cons of the argument I had set out to win, that she wanted to risk the time and energy on the old story of "us."

I stumbled upon success by accident. I became convinced that she was right and I was wrong. There was no logical reason for her to give us another try. It seemed to me that she had clearly won the argument. I gave up. I was in no happy state. I sat back, totally drained, no longer arguing. I must have seemed calm on the surface. There *was* a funny kind of very empty calm within, a feeling of resignation, what I imagine a person who has just fallen out of an airplane ten miles up who realizes there's no way he can save himself must feel. I let go. But the logic of the inevitable impact that follows a fall does not always apply to love. You see, in this resigned state, I was on a kind of automatic pilot, listening to what my lover was saying, even helping her to clarify her points without arguing. Then I finally noticed it seemed to be important to her to say certain things. I encouraged her rather than arguing with her. As we left the restaurant, almost as an afterthought, I asked, "Well, would you prefer that I just go away and disappear from your life, or would you like me to maintain contact?" "Oh, to maintain contact," she said. That was all I needed. From then on I knew how to discuss differences of opinion—you do it in a manner that shows you care not just for your own opinion but also for the person with whom you are discussing your opinion.

MODERN-DAY BEN FRANKLIN

The Benjamin Franklin Technique is meant to maintain relationships, not win arguments. If you genuinely believe you are right, then convincing the other person of the proper point of view should be handled as just another aspect of loving. If despite your original belief, you discover you were wrong, or not completely right, rather than lose, you become convinced of a better way. Discussion becomes a "You-win/I-win" situation. The technique takes time to learn. It may seem to go against one's natural inclination, especially in the emotionally charged arguments that sometimes occur between lovers, and most of all when you feel hurt and angered by your lover's rejection.

Here's how to use the Ben Franklin Technique when your ex-lover needs to criticize or argue with you. First, *find points of agreement.* This will immediately take the wind out of the sails of a full-scale argument. Second, *state points of disagreement as if you could agree perhaps under other circumstances,* but under these circumstances you think otherwise.

The surprise of a conciliatory assertion can give pause to an angry mind.

Example

After a long hard day you undress and step into the shower. You lather up, lose yourself in the sounds and the soothing flow of hot water, which carry away the aches and exertions of the day. Suddenly on the other side of the curtain you hear your lover say, "Hey, what are you doing? Don't use up all the goddamn hot water. I want to take a shower later."

You happen to know that there's plenty of hot water left. In fact, you could leave the hot water on all night and there'd be some left. You *could,* prefacing your remarks with a few expletives, shout that fact at your lover, and demonstrate it later by leaving the hot water on all night, but then, perhaps winning an argument about hot water is not the point. So instead you might stick your head out from behind the curtain and smile, saying, "Oh, I'm sorry, hon, I don't want to take your hot shower away from you." (Point of agreement.) "But, you know, in our other apartment it was true, we had to worry about how much hot water we had, but I don't think we have to in this building." (Point of disagreement with which under other circumstances you could have agreed.) You might even add, along with your smile, "Why don't you join me?"

DEFUSING ANGER AND THE PORCUPINE TECHNIQUE

What happens if, despite your efforts to Ben Franklin your lover (and yourself) into arguing without getting too angry or emotional, the anger does get out of hand? *Do not respond in kind to obscene language* or name-calling.

Though you sometimes may feel this kind of behavior is necessary to get attention or to show that you mean business, in truth, the primary purpose of these maneuvers is to inflict psychic pain, and the likely result of using them is to increase your ex-lover's use of them in turn, in an attempt to hurt you more than you hurt him. If you feel you must use an obscenity to emphasize a point, then take care that it is not directed at your beloved but is used solely as an emphasizer—"Damn it, don't you know I love you?" not "Damn you, don't you know I love you?"

Even if your ex-lover is the first to hurl an outrageous obscenity and you are the target, if you want to save your love-bond, allow your lover to wallow in his or her own obscenities. For example, in the shower scene above, one of the options was to respond without using expletives. Stand firm on principle, but remain polite in style. Your angry lover will become increasingly uncomfortable with his own obnoxiousness, and unless you are dealing with an impaired lover (see chapter 10), will cease off-the-wall unreasonableness. This manner of handling anger is based on a thoroughly tested, well-known salesperson's technique, called the Porcupine Technique.

A salesperson is in a similar position to a rejected lover. If he is to be successful, he has to keep in mind that his purpose is to make a sale, not to out-insult his customer. A rejected lover wants to convince a former lover to reconsider a relationship. Exchanging angry insults is not likely to accomplish this. Instead of responding to obnoxious behavior by being obnoxious himself, the salesperson calmly and politely refutes or, if appropriate, concurs with hostile assertions—anger is turned against the customer in the same way that the blows (or bites) of an attacker against a porcupine inflict more pain on the attacker than on the nonaggressive, but sharply defensive porcupine.

In my psychiatric practice I often coach my patients on

how to handle arguments with their lovers. When they learn not to respond to anger with anger, they observe that disagreement loses the aura of combat.

Ida's husband, Jim, was changing the car's oil. She acted as his assistant, taking the orders that he barked at her, as was her custom and his expectation whenever there was any project around the house. Whenever she'd make a mistake, he'd eagerly jump on it, telling her what an idiot she was. She would wait for him to make mistakes so that she could do the same to him. Their relationship became a dueling match of sarcastic humor. Since they had been in a "love"-bond for some time, they knew just how to chip away at each other's self-esteem. Chronic underlying unhappiness and resentment were building up. Ida noticed a threadbare tire on the car. She said, "Hey, lunkhead, that tire's had it. Why don't you change it?"

He said in response, "Nothing's wrong with that goddamned tire. You don't know what you're talking about, as usual."

"Okay," she said. "Whatever . . ."

The next day the tire went flat. In a therapy session Ida related the incident to me as if she had achieved a great success. I asked her, "What really had been accomplished?" Yes, she had managed to put him in *his* place, assuming being the target of well-aimed ridicule was his place. But did that really help their relationship? Would it end the war that was going on between them?

Ida loved Jim and she wanted him to love her the way he had when they got married. But she was losing him. She thought that by being "right" about the tire he would come around to seeing she was worth listening to. But people, especially lovers, don't work that way. Jim needed to be loved, not convinced, and the defensive name-calling only increased the distance between them.

I suggested Ida try a combination of Ben Franklin and

the Porcupine in order to love Jim back to her. It wasn't easy, the pattern was firmly established, but she saw how self-defeating it was. Whenever he'd make mistakes, she eventually learned not to respond automatically with "See what a jerk you are?" or the equivalent. When he cursed or barked at her, she turned into a porcupine and did not curse or bark at him but simply responded to the issue at hand. She'd compliment him on what he had done right and make tentative suggestions. In time he relaxed a bit. She became less critical and expressed genuine delight in his accomplishments.

Now she tells him when he does or says things that hurt her feelings, and she can be quite firm about it, but she does not (at least not as often) attempt to hurt him in kind. So their relationship has improved.

To be sure, the pleasures of ego-crunching are hard for some people to resist. Bobby Fischer, former world-champion chess player, used to speak of the pleasure of sensing the crunch of his opponent's ego when the game's decisive move was made. Many people would flinch at admitting to such a pleasure—in arguments between lovers, the desire to ego-crunch is often veiled by rationalizations, for example, "I had to make my point." Ben Franklin would have recognized the folly of such a contention.

Points can be made, and in fact made more effectively, without humiliating your lover. It simply doesn't make sense to inflict pyschological pain deliberately on someone with whom you hope to have a meaningful relationship. The relationship will suffer, and so will you.

USING YOUR LOVER'S ANGER

If you can learn to stay calm and to defuse your lover's anger, you will probably find harsh realities underneath it. Coping with and learning from those realities will win your lover back to you *and* help you learn about yourself.

You will notice in our example above that the cause of hostility between Ida and her husband was not really disagreement about particular issues, as, for example, whether or not the tire was about to go, but the self-destructive game of putting each other down. Even if they could come to an agreement on a particular issue, the pattern of hostile disagreement would have continued. They would have found other things to fight about.

Anger is always about something, but the stated issue may not be the real cause of your lover's anger. For example, one of the classic symptoms of the impending breakup of a relationship is angry arguments over what previously seemed insignificant. You have always left the toothpaste out; now that becomes an issue. If your lover is secretly having an affair, perhaps his new lover is contrasted with you by the little courtesies she shows—like putting the toothpaste away. I do not mean to belittle the significance of considerate gestures like putting toothpaste away or the toilet seat down, but if these or other similar issues suddenly take on a *major* significance when previously they went ignored, the real issue may be a basic dissatisfaction with the relationship, and the real issue ought to be ferreted out, so that it can be dealt with. One of the insanities of arguments between dissatisfied lovers is that even if the argument itself is resolved, the arguing persists because the real, underlying issue has not been resolved.

In your search for the real issue, be prepared to deal with it when you uncover it.

Tracey noticed that her boyfriend, Blaine, had become distant and irritable. She knew that his old girlfriend, Colette, had returned to town. Tracey had insisted and Blaine had agreed not to make any attempt to see Colette.

One day Tracey approached him and told him he could talk openly, that she sensed that something was wrong. He looked at her suspiciously. She said, "It's okay. I understand. It's important that we be able to talk about these things. You miss her, don't you?" He suddenly appreciated Tracey in a way he had never appreciated her before, but as soon as he said the words "Yes, I do miss Colette . . . ," Tracey exploded in anger, hysterically screeching, "You bastard! Why don't you just go back to her then!"

This was part of Tracey's pattern of jealously guarding her love-bond. Blaine did not go back to Colette, but his relationship with Tracey did not last long. She uncovered the issue, but she was not willing to deal with it.

If there is a problem or potential disagreement that needs to be discussed, allow your lover to state his view on the matter. Wait until he has completed his remarks. Give his views a full and careful hearing, even if they're upsetting. Ask for permission to state your own view. Do not attempt to read his mind. If you think that you might know something that is going on inside your lover's head, ask permission to speculate or at least acknowledge that you are speculating.

A note on mind reading: mind reading is a very unrewarding habit in relationships. Your lover may come to expect you to do it, to know what he is upset about, in which case you will be constantly trying to guess what is wrong. When you are wrong about what's wrong, your lover may get all the angrier and accuse you of being insensitive.

The situation could become even worse if you get *good* at mind reading. People don't appreciate it if you've got them so well figured out that you can tell them what they're thinking. Admit that you're speculating when you guess at someone else's concern, even if you are usually right. When you are successful at loving, the person you love will continue to grow intellectually and emotionally, and you will never be able to assume that you know exactly what is going on.

In the example of Tracey and Blaine, Tracey starts out quite well—an understanding tone, an acknowledged speculation about what might be bothering Blaine, asking him to speak, making it clear that she is ready to understand his point of view, his feeling, but then she blows it by getting caught up in her own anger and closing down the possibility of any reasonable discussion. She is not really prepared to deal with the underlying cause of Blaine's moodiness. She would have been better off had she not even attempted it, because now Blaine can no longer trust her to handle an honest expression of feelings. Without that, they will get caught in an endless series of surface arguments—whose turn it is to wash the dishes, what program on TV to watch—it doesn't matter what the issue, they will fight about it.

THE FINE ART OF THE LOVING TAKE-AWAY

Using the conciliatory or calming techniques we've been discussing does not mean that you must put up with behavior you find demeaning or otherwise repugnant. The line between loving and manipulating is crossed when you find yourself accepting behavior you find unacceptable—have the self-awareness and self-respect not to cross that line. Part of loving is setting limits on the behavior of those we love, for loving 100 percent means being honest, not manipulative. One of the most effective ways of setting limits is the take-away. It can be used to handle unreasonable verbal assault; it can also be used if, despite shared positive moments, your lover seems to take you for granted.

Adults must often set limits on one another. Without limits there is a tendency for the most sober-minded and mature to become unreasonable. As Lord Acton said: "Power tends to corrupt and absolute power corrupts absolutely." This is as true within the context of adult romantic relationships as it is in politics. No matter how special, wonderful, loving, or beautiful your lover may be; no matter how desperate for love you are; you must retain the ability to say no. This is especially true in a love-bond where, because of the tendency to glamorize and become emotionally dependent on the beloved, you may tend to tolerate grossly unreasonable, even pathological behavior.

"Love is blind," goes the old saying. Obscured by the "limerant" glow that often precedes and accompanies a love-bond, your lover may seem beyond the pale of normal human limitation, but if your lover has a heart that beats and blood that flows, he must occasionally be reminded that his is not the only will in the world.

In the first chapter of this book, I suggested that you not sacrifice financial or physical well-being in the process of getting your lover back—that if you did so, you would actually decrease the chance of success. This is one kind of limit setting. The fine art of the loving take-away is another. This art not only protects your own self-interest, it helps you toward your goal of getting your lover back.

At its most effective, the take-away is done gently, even lovingly. Salespeople often use it. If you would like to see a crude application of the take-away, go to a health spa you don't belong to and inquire about the cost of membership. In one way or another you will be told that if you buy a membership *today*—you will always happen to come in on *the day*—it will be cheaper than if you buy tomorrow, so you'd better act now or a special opportunity will be taken away from you. The take-away may even be used in the physical act of offering you a contract. The paper is pushed toward you, but the salesperson's hand still gently rests on it, the overt and implied possibility of losing this "golden opportunity," this "special deal," this "Memorial Day weekend," "Fourth of July," or "Labor Day special," remains.

If the potential buyer is a simple, nonresistant soul, or someone who has had a few drinks, then placing the pen in the buyer's hand and saying "Sign!" may be enough. But this coercion will increase the likelihood that the buyer will come back (perhaps with an enraged spouse or relative) and demand a refund and cancellation of the deal.

When you are selling yourself to your lover, it is important that your lover feel loved, even when you use the take-away technique. The take-away should not be wielded as a heavy-handed threat that appears more like extortion than love.

If Matt demanded of Inge, "You stop seeing that jerk Zeke or we're finished," he would be using an ineffective version of the take-away. Also he would have to bear in mind that if he makes a threat, he must be willing to follow through on it, or else, by the second or third time he makes it, he will lose whatever remaining credibility he has, becoming analogous to the child who cried wolf. It is best not to make a threat at all, or to make it so that it does not seem like a threat. A reasonable, calm "either-or" can bring certain facts to the attention of an ex-lover. You need to remember that the take-away is done not to hurt and not out of a desire for vengeance, but out of calm necessity, because you find you honestly cannot go on being the one who is forever understanding, forever *there,* ultimately taken for granted, a puppet on strings to your ex-lover, not commanding any respect, and therefore not likely to get respect or love.

In a simple case an ex-lover will respond to a few pleasant experiences and then decide to give the relationship another chance, and you will have him or her back. In a more difficult case, though rapport and communication may improve, an ex-lover may not be so quick to return. Pleasant experiences without commitment may go on indefinitely. If what you want is the commitment of a love-bond, and your ex-lover is slow to return, the time comes when it feels necessary to try the take-away. When do you do this? Trust your instincts. The take-away works best when you legitimately feel you cannot continue the way things are.

The take-away will accomplish two things: (a) It will speed up an ex-lover's return; and (b) it will help establish equality in a relationship.

If she or he persists in taking you for granted, *use the take-away lovingly.* If he or she is in the midst of a career-determining business deal, or is about to open an art exhibit, or is involved in some other major issue, then be flexible with the scheduling of joint time. Just as loving yourself by not sacrificing livelihood or health is important, loving your ex-lover requires you not to expect him to sacrifice livelihood or health.

No matter how insistent your declaration of eternal love, the longer your ex-lover takes to return to you, the greater the risk that *you* will lose interest, that *you* will eventually meet someone else. That risk is implicit, but obvious. Rarely would anyone need to state it.

When you first reestablished contact, you used every opportunity available to create positive moments. If, between the times that you spent with your ex-lover, you continued with your life, went to work, spent time with friends, pursued hobbies, then you have established the framework for a successful take-away. Your ex-lover should realize that you are there for him if he decides to come back to you, but that your life will not stop. This can be said to him, but your action is what counts the most. In fact, if your ex-lover has any psychological sophistication at all, repeated statements that your life will go on even if it be without him will be perceived as proof of the opposite. An ex-lover could ask, "Are you trying to convince yourself?"

So say "I love you, and I will wait for you, but I am going on with my life" only when the occasion arises. Regardless of whether you say it or not, both you and your ex-lover know that while you wait, you could meet someone else and that you may not wait forever. Then, after the framework has been established, you begin to make yourself a little less available. You don't refuse time with him, you just don't allocate all your free time to him, and you begin to increase the priority of other people and projects in your life. In this way you are, by your action, reminding your ex-lover that though you love him, he doesn't have absolute power over you and therefore cannot take you for granted. This is *the primary take-away*. It is initiated by you. At its heart is self-restraint. You are no longer throwing your love at your ex-lover. Your love is obvious but becomes more understated. Your self-love and self-sufficiency are more apparent, and those qualities will make you very attractive.

Amateurs in the art of observing relationships sometimes say that men really desire only women who are difficult to win and vice versa, that it is the challenge that people are looking for in relationships. This is only superficially true. Below the surface is the reality that self-loving, self-sufficient people are the most attractive potential partners in romance. Why? Because when you're loved by a self-loving person, you know you're being loved because you're you, not because you're someone who can meet the insecure person's need to be loved. A person who plays at being hard to get can give the appearance of self-assurance and self-love, but eventually intimacy cuts through the lie.

If you only *seem* to have these qualities, then you have not established the framework for a successful take-away.

The *secondary take-away* can be used as a countermove to an ex-lover's direct or implied threat of a take-away. For example, if Inge says that Zeke wants her to move to Colorado with him and then she looks at Matt as if waiting to see what he will do next (perhaps go berserk?), Matt might calmly say, "I hope you don't. I love you one hundred percent, but I realize that you have to decide what you want to do."

By exercising self-restraint, Matt is using a take-away. If he attempted to grasp her by insisting that she not go, he would either chase her away or, if she decided to stay, give her incredible power over him (and he would then never be secure in his relationship with her).

There is an additional advantage to self-restraint. So long as Matt remains calm, even pointing out advantages, along with the disadvantages of a move to Colorado, he enhances his value as a listener. Inge discovers that she is able to confide in him. If she comes to value him as her confidant, then she will grow ever closer to him. He should remind her from time to time that he loves her, that he wants her, but also that because he loves her, he wants her to consider all her options. If she decides that she wants to come back to him, he wants the decision to be 100 percent. He demonstrates considerable strength in using this approach. In reality, he is doing a Loving Take-Away. Loving Take-Aways have considerable tugging power.

By the way, if she is just testing her power over him by threatening him with a move to Colorado, he has taught her that power plays don't work. She may even get angry at him if she's in the habit of confusing dependency with love. By demonstrating the difference to her, he could be helping her to see the difference and therefore truly loving her.

An Example of a Take-Away

Inge and Matt have now shared many pleasant dates together. They are seeing each other frequently. Matt even suspects that she has canceled a date with Zeke in order to be with him this evening.

They are in one of those pizza places with long wooden tables, and scuffed wooden floors. The scuffings enhance the casual atmosphere—just the right place for eating pizza and drinking beer. He remembers his days as a college student when he might have taken out a penknife to commemorate the occasion into the wood. He wonders what it would have been like to share those days with Inge and thinks of asking *her* thoughts on the matter.

They sit across from each other at the end of one of the long tables. Looking up from her menu, she asks, "What do you want?"

"Let's split a medium-sized pizza, thin crust, with everything but the anchovies."

"That's not what I meant," she says, laughing, as if relieved that he had not answered her intended question. "And what's wrong with anchovies anyway?"

"Oh, what did you mean? Did you want them?" He's ready to tell her that he may not want the anchovies, but he does want her, if that's what her question comes to.

"No, just kidding." She smiles, avoiding the intended topic for a moment.

The beer is brought right away, and they begin to drink it. While they wait for the pizza, just as Matt is feeling aglow and relaxed and about to reflect on what it might have been like had he and Inge been college students together, Inge interrupts his thoughts: "Matt, I know you think you've got me back. We've been spending a lot of time together, and it's been noticed on the other end too. I mean, Zeke has noticed it, too, but I'm just as confused as ever about what I want to do. I don't mean to get you upset. I know you were feeling good."

"No. You have to say what you feel." He's not sure that he believes her confusion. Perhaps she just thinks she is confused. The outward signs of a decision in his favor are obvious. He wonders if she feels guilty about what is happening to Zeke.

"You don't look happy," she says.

"Well, of course, I'm disappointed. I *did* have the impression that you were coming closer to my view of us."

"I know. But it's not really Zeke's fault that his apartment is small, and I get kind of claustrophobic at times."

Matt cannot help but feel inward delight on hearing this.

She continues. "You know how I am sometimes. I get moody and I just feel a need for space, but it's not his fault. He didn't know me when he rented that apartment. Just because you're renting a house and I feel more comfortable there. . . . Those kinds of physical conveniences aren't what a decision about a relationship should be based on."

"Of course not." Is this the argument Zeke has been using on her? Is she testing Zeke's argument on him?

"It's easier to spend time with you, because it's more convenient. Do you think I should come back to you because it's more convenient?"

"Are you coming back to me because it's more convenient?"

"No, but I don't know if I want to come back."

He says abruptly, "Maybe you should spend more time with Zeke."

"Well," she says, irritation entering her voice, "if you're not interested anymore, that's fine." She sighs as if relieved.

He fears he has been too abrupt. He says in a steady

voice, "I love you, and if you're confused about what to do, I think you should take the time or do whatever you have to do to get unconfused. Naturally I would prefer that you not see Zeke at all, but I love you and I don't want you to come back to me confused." *A gentle take-away.*

"You understand, then?"

"Yes, I understand. I want you to stay here with me to live happily ever after, but I even think that if going to Colorado is what would get you unconfused, then that is what you should do."

She says, pleasantly enough, half talking to herself, "I don't need to hear that from you."

"I want to wait for you. Is that all right with you, or would you prefer that I get out of your life altogether?"

"I never said that I wanted you out of my life."

"Good. I'll wait, then, sweetpea."

As if on cue, the waitress arrives with their pizza.

He says, "You know, I was thinking it would have been fun if I had met you when I was going to college, but then you would have still been in grammar school."

"It still might have been fun."

He laughs.

A month prior to their conversation over pizza, he had asked her if she would like to go with him to a jazz concert on April 19. She had looked sad when she said, "I'm sorry. I've already been asked."

One month after their conversation over pizza, they spent the afternoon of April 19 together. Matt pulled into a parking space in front of Zeke's apartment to drop her off.

She asked, "Would you like to get together this evening?"

"I thought you were going to the concert with Zeke."

"You remember that?"

"Of course."

She smiled at him. She was getting out of the car. He

said, "You are going in there to pick a fight with him so that you can cancel the concert date and call me, aren't you?"

"Quit it." She laughed. She walked toward the apartment building and waved as she closed the iron gate behind her.

He drove off with a sense of triumph, but couldn't help wondering if she was really going to deliberately pick a fight with Zeke. If she was, that would seem to be a good thing, but it would also indicate a character trait to be borne in mind for future reference.

That night she did call, and they made love and then slept together. The next morning he asked, "I've got you back, don't I?"

"You know you do."

Victory, or so he thought.

Chapter 10

LOVING IMPAIRED LOVERS, AND WHY PEOPLE BOTHER

THE TEMPTATION TO GET INVOLVED (AGAIN) WITH AN IMPAIRED LOVER

Several years ago Becky's two-year romance with Eric ended. She still thinks of that time with an intense nostalgic longing and often wonders if their relationship could have turned out differently, or "Is it true that relationships that don't work shouldn't work?"

Becky found a new job as a nurse, and once again Eric is in her life. He is now a surgeon at the hospital where Becky works. They immediately strike up a friendship, reminiscing about old acquaintances and old times. In her heart she is somewhat disappointed to hear that he is living with a new lover, but he says he is happy, and so she smiles and says, "That's good."

She enjoys her renewed, this time platonic, friendship with him. Their work on the same ward at the hospital brings them together from time to time. She admires the work he does, the range of his intellect, and still finds him incredibly good-looking. She wonders, if she had been more understanding during their time together several years ago, would she now be in a wonderfully happy romance with him, instead of alone? Sure, she dates, but "there just don't seem to be any really eligible men who have their act together."

One day Eric joins Becky at the nursing station for a cup of coffee. They discuss one of their mutual patients for a while, but then Eric changes the tone of the conversation. "Becky, you and I almost made it work one time. I still miss you." He looks at her.

She knows without saying anything that her eyes tell him she's interested. He's got to be able to tell by the way she talks and acts whenever he's around that she is still attracted to him. She feels excited. She smiles.

He says, "Mary and I have been having a rough time lately. I don't think it's going to work out with us. She's out of town with her parents this weekend. You want to get together?"

"Does she know you'll be seeing someone else?"

"No, of course not."

Perhaps Eric *is* on the verge of breaking up with Mary, and if Becky spends some time with him now, she might expedite things, might bring him back to her. She still loves him. However, he's revealed a disturbing trait. He's dishonest with Mary. How does Becky know he's not dishonest with her as well?

Becky could say she's interested but insist that he settle things with Mary before starting something new. This way she lets him know that honesty is important to her. Eric's dishonesty may not be a deeply ingrained trait, and if Becky insists on honesty in her relationship with him, she may love him free of the relationship-imparing quality of dishonesty.

What, however, if Eric's dishonesty is a recurrent theme

in his interactions with women? Suppose part of the story of his original breakup with Becky was that he had secretly had affairs with various nurses and ward clerks at the hospital, eventually becoming attached to one and leaving Becky altogether. Then Eric is an impaired lover. He's dishonest. Unless he shows a convincing and consistent change in behavior, not just in words, Becky is on notice that Eric simply lacks the ability to maintain his end of a love-bond.

If Becky finds herself ignoring her own insight into Eric's dishonesty, or perhaps making excuses for it, then she is not loving her lover, nor is she loving herself. She's facilitating his dishonesty, encouraging his impaired relationship style; and she's subjecting herself to the long-term misery of a relationship that just won't work. If she's so needy as to tolerate a partner in a love-bond who cannot love her back, because of his dishonesty, then she's too needy to be in a relationship. She herself is probably impaired. She is certainly not loving.

Romantic love-bonds are not charity work. They require people who love themselves first, who are honest, and who are capable of making a commitment to love someone else.

THE IMPAIRED LOVER

The impaired lover comes in many varieties, but the basic characteristic is that he is stuck in a particular mode of behavior that by its nature, at least part of the time, interferes with his ability to love.

Note the significance of the word *stuck*. Most of us waver in our relationship skills from time to time. Even a concert pianist sometimes doesn't play well, but if he's got a terrible habit that interferes with his playing, say, going on drunken binges or throwing temper tantrums in which he destroys his piano, then pretty soon he's no longer a piano player, and a lover with similar habits is no longer a lover. Sometimes such people can change, but one should never believe the change has occurred until consistent evidence of the change in behavior is seen.

In evaluating whether or not your lover is impaired, you should ask the following basic questions:

- Is your lover basically honest?
- Is your lover basically secure within himself?
- Could your lover survive without you? (Being very sad if you were no longer in his life is not the same as not being able to survive.)
- Can your lover communicate feelings and thoughts through some means—words? touch? facial expression? body stance?
- Does your lover show evidence of understanding what you feel, what you say?
- Does he demonstrate interest in what you feel, what you say?
- Does he encourage you in the development of interests that make you feel alive?
- Does he say when he disagrees with you?
- Does he allow you to disagree with him?
- Does he maintain his respect for self and others when under stress?

A persistent no to any one of these questions indicates that your lover lacks part of the basic psychological makeup needed to maintain a love-bond. To that extent he's impaired. He's "stuck" in a behavior pattern or patterns that make a love-bond with him especially difficult, just as a person who is out of breath after walking half a block is going to find running a marathon especially difficult (unless he begins a serious effort to get in shape).

If the answer to each of these questions is generally yes, then your lover has the personality characteristics for handling a love-bond (he's in shape, just as a runner who is about to run a marathon ought to be in shape). You'll notice that these questions deal with very basic issues, so that a persistent no is pretty convincing evidence of serious impairment. There may be times when you are not sure how persistent the no is, but by asking the question you've identified the problem area and can be alert to it. If you are successfully loving someone, you may love him or her into becoming a capable (nonimpaired) lover, but you've got to see evidence of change.

HOW DO PEOPLE END UP IN RELATIONSHIPS WITH IMPAIRED LOVERS?

First of all, *they ignore the evidence.* Part of the blame for this is the falling-in-love or "limerance" response that often precedes the establishment of a love-bond. As already mentioned in chapter 2, the sexual-emotional attraction that is the substance of "falling in love" can be very intense. The mind goes into a kind of trance state in which the positive qualities of the love-object are exaggerated, or even created out of nothing and projected onto the love-object by the imagination, while the negative qualities are given little significance or ignored altogether. Perception of reality is distorted by the trance. In fact, if losing contact with reality is the essence of insanity, then, by definition, people who fall in love are at least partially insane. "He's crazy over her" is closer to truth than it is to metaphor.

This distortion of reality that takes place in the mind of the romantic was observed over a hundred years ago by the poet-philosopher Friedrich Nietzsche, who described it in his book *Joyful Science* (#60, "Women and Their Effect at a Distance"):

Here stand I in the midst of the passionate surf whose white flames lick at my feet—from all sides howls, screams, and shrill cries come at me. . . . Then suddenly . . . appears . . . a large sailing vessel, gliding as silent as a spirit. . . . Oh, the spiritual beauty! With what magic it seizes me! . . . Does all the peace and stillness of the world sail with you? Does my happiness reside in [your] quiet place, my happy self, my second, eternal self . . . [with] the ship which with its white sails moves like a large butterfly over the dark sea. . . . If a man stands in the midst of his own noise, in the midst of the passion of his projects and plans, from there, he sees well the quiet, magical beings that glide by after whose happiness and seclusion, he longs—these beings are women. . . . However, noble dreamer, there is also on the most beautiful sailing vessel so much clamor and noise and sadly so much small, pitiful noise! The magic and most powerful effect of women is . . . an effect at a distance.

The same can be said of men.

The distance and the imagined calm allow a romantic to project fantasies and to fall in love. When intimacy closes the gap of distance, reality once again asserts itself, and the beloved is no longer what he or she seemed to be. The good part is that the vision of perfection that comes with falling in love can create faith in the potential of the love-bond, and real loving can begin. The bad part is that one can become enamored with the vision and deny or rationalize away the traits of a lover that don't fit the vision. If the reality of the beloved's imperfections is not serious and persistent, then they can be lived with, perhaps changed, but if persistent and serious, then we must admit the discovery that we are in love with an impaired lover.

In the opening scenario of this chapter, Becky may so enjoy the positive qualities of Eric that she will rationalize away or deny his dishonesty so that she can hold on to her romantic vision. However, in time, his dishonesty, if persistent, will force itself upon her. "Love is blind," but the pain an impaired lover inflicts upon you is real.

It is easy enough for a relationship to go well in the controlled setting of a date over the glow of sparkling wine with waiters and waitresses taking care of you, perhaps with a good view and a fine meal. What if, on the way to the restaurant, the car breaks down? Your lover begins to curse, perhaps to punch the car, maybe even snaps at you. Your lover is demonstrating how he handles stress. Watch and learn. You are witnessing how the stressful times that test most relationships will be handled.

Is your lover discourteous, perhaps threatening to others? In a long-term relationship, do you really think you will be immune to these traits of his? Is that acceptable to you?

Don't let the glow of falling in love blind you to traits that may cause you pain. Do not ignore the evidence.

Perhaps the commitment of your lover to his profession impressed you to the point of admiration when you first met, but if you begin to notice that your doctor-, lawyer-, musician-lover never has time for you, other than those times when you are admiring what he does, then don't rationalize away this significant bit of evidence. So many frustrated lovers keep waiting for something to happen, that is, for a little attention to be directed their way. Their lover's work is so impressive that they hesitate to ask for time. But a relationship is impaired unless there is time spent on it. You cannot make your lover spend time on it. When his admiration society—you—begins the Loving

Take-Away, perhaps he will come around, but there are people who are "married" to their career. Is it okay with you if your lover is that way? You decide. You owe it to yourself not to ignore the evidence.

Then again a lover may inordinately resent your chosen career. An actress began to notice that whenever she was offered a choice role, her boyfriend said it wasn't right for her. He was adamant that she not take "these roles." He said that his "concern" was "for her." Finally the actress realized that she was losing significant opportunities for recognition in regional theater. Her boyfriend became increasingly angry with her as she began to accept roles and became publicly recognized as an actress. If there was an article about her or a picture of her in the newspaper, he became so irritable that she found it very unpleasant to be around him.

If we remember the definition of love discussed in chapter 2—"the active concern for the life and growth of the person loved"—her boyfriend ought to be encouraging her potential, not discouraging it. She can attempt to discuss the issue with him, reassure him she loves him, devote time to their relationship, but if his jealousy persists, then he is too impaired to be in a relationship with her. If she compromises by giving up a vital interest, a potential way of experiencing life that makes her profoundly happy, then she is allowing herself to be injured, not loved. By giving into his jealousy she would be loving neither her lover nor herself. Is she so dependent on this one person that she must tolerate his impaired form of love? This brings us to the second reason people find themselves in relationships with impaired lovers.

People end up in relationships with impaired lovers because *they themselves are impaired.*

When you realize that your partner is too severely impaired and/or is not willing to make the effort to change, you may find that he or she becomes less attractive to you. There may be sadness, but you move on, as you realize your partner lacks the prerequisites for handling a love-bond. If you rationalize remaining in an impaired relationship, then aren't you deliberately choosing to be unhappy? And if unhappiness is your choice, then perhaps you should ask yourself the same basic questions you asked in evaluating whether or not your lover is impaired (see page 178). Are you an impaired lover?

Angela had discovered that her boyfriend, Todd, was lying about attending business meetings. Really he was having an affair with Lisa. Finally Todd announced that he was leaving Angela in order to move in with Lisa. Todd claimed, "Well, I was telling the truth. There *were* these business meetings. I didn't know I was suddenly going to fall in love."

Angela was devastated. She cried and begged and kept calling Todd up on the phone. She came to me for advice. I coached her in the various strategies of this book. Within a matter of two months Todd was again expressing interest in her. He finally admitted to her that he had been wrong in lying to her (for so long!). She was hopeful, but then every time he apologized, he'd conclude with, "But you have to admit, it was at least half your fault that I lied to you." (He did this several times.) He just wouldn't *really* accept that his lying was inappropriate. Angela began to wonder if he was lying to Lisa. Was he not telling Lisa that he was seeing his old girlfriend Angela? When she discovered that he had practiced similar deceit in previous relationships, she was angry at first, but then she saw it as a kind of persistent impairment that rendered him incapable of functioning in an honest romance. (You can't expect a turnip seed to grow a tomato.) She lost interest in him as a potential partner in romance. Had she continued in a relationship with him, she would have been showing signs of being an impaired lover herself. To tolerate abuse—and chronic deceit without evidence of change is abuse—would mean that she did not love herself, that is, that she herself lacked one of the prerequisites for successful participation in a love-bond.

The underlying cause of someone who knowingly tolerates the chronic misery of "romantic" involvement with an impaired lover is lack of self-love, which translates into something like: "I can't leave him. If I do, I won't have anybody. This is the best I can do. A person with his positive qualities, without the negative, wouldn't want me." This is a no-win situation, because a relationship between impaired lovers by definition won't work. Woody Allen expressed the dilemma well: "I wouldn't want to join a club that would accept me for a member." The only lovers acceptable to someone who lacks self-love are unacceptable as lovers. If you're in this pattern, you need to work on learning to love youself before you begin to try to make a relationship work. Remember, you have to be in psychological shape to handle a relationship.

A common variant of this pattern of knowingly staying in a relationship with an impaired lover is playing the role of the savior. The Savior Syndrome is the desire to demonstrate one's own worth by saving others. If one had a sense of self-worth (a consequence of self-love) to start with, the syndrome wouldn't develop.

A desire to save people, especially in the less intense form of "helping," rather than saving, has its positive aspects. So long as a person recognizes the limits of what can be done, and does not allow himself to be abused, especially in certain professional roles such as medical doctor and teacher, a "helping" style of behavior is admirable. However, if the desire to help others has become a *need*, and if that need has crept into one's relationship pattern, then genuine love ceases to be a possibility. One becomes threatened if one's lover "improves" and no longer needs help—the relationship by its very nature becomes based on "sickness."

The Savior Syndrome can take on extreme forms. Let's look at an example: In John Cheever's short story "Torch Song," Joan Harris knows only one kind of relationship. Protagonist Jack Lorey "began to think of her as the Widow. She always wore black, and he was always given the feeling, by a curious disorder in her apartment, that the undertakers had just left." Jack has known her for years. He meets her from time to time at a party or shares drinks with her at a restaurant. She has kept him informed of her long series of relationships. All of her lovers suffer from some major problem of one kind or another, including alcoholism. Then the day comes when Jack's own problems catch up with him: He has lost two jobs, is forced to pay alimony to two ex-wives, can afford nothing better than a dump to live in, and is sinking ever deeper into illness and excessive drinking. Joan shows up at his doorstep.

"Jack tried to sit up in bed, as if there were some need to defend himself, and then fell back again, against the pillows. . . .'You know, you've never come to a place of mine before—never,' he said. 'Why did you come now?' "

Insight comes to him. He resents her implied prognosis.

" 'Get out,' he said again, and when she didn't move, he shouted, 'What kind of an obscenity are you that you can smell sickness and death the way you do?' " He insists that his "life isn't ending" and sarcastically promises to call her when "the wonderful years ahead" of him are "over, when it's time."

She has to leave to go to work, but promises to come back that night. His sarcasms have no effect on her. She's experienced far worse—beatings by drunks, vile verbal abuse, loss of an apartment and nearly her job because of her sick boyfriends—all part of the self-imposed suffering that is part of the Savior Syndrome.

Jack so desperately wishes to escape her that he might even recover—which would be the end of their relationship. He demonstrates a degree of strength not evidenced by her former lovers—despite his problems, he escapes his "savior's" neediness. She remains impaired, looking for an impaired lover with whom to get involved. She is not really interested in a romantic love-bond, and those who are would avoid her kind of "romance."

You can change an unimpaired lover into an impaired lover, if you don't set limits on inappropriate behavior. Part of loving someone is reminding them when they are beginning to develop habits of inconsiderate behavior. The best remedy against this is to keep communication open.

For example, suppose one Friday evening you decide to surprise your lover by preparing an especially nice gourmet dinner. You do this not because it is expected, nor is it part of your normal routine together; you just want to surprise the one you love with something pleasant. He's pleased and thanks you, and you have a wonderful evening together. You prepare similar dinners the next couple of Fridays, but then on the fourth Friday, you're tired, and so you decide not to. He becomes angry. "Where the hell's dinner!?" Now, if you love him, you tell him you are tired and not in the mood, and you remind him that you prepared those dinners as a gift, not an obligation. Perhaps he will still be angry, but it is important to draw the line. Otherwise, he begins to take you for granted, and the pattern of taking you for granted could begin to affect more and more aspects of your life together, which would mean a steady drift in the direction of an impaired relationship. If new patterns of behavior are caught early, they are relatively easy to change. Please note that we are talking "patterns." Probably all of us are at least occasionally inappropriate—that's when we rely on our friends and lovers to remind us that we are being inconsiderate (showing evidence of a new negative pattern). When the habit of good communication is firmly established, the reminding occurs naturally.

An already impaired relationship can become more impaired if new bad habits (negative patterns of behavior) are not caught early. Mary Ann was seeing a psychiatrist because of depression and anxiety that she felt were related to her husband's "problem with alcohol." She had jumped into a marriage with an alcoholic boyfriend to escape an intolerable life with alcoholic parents. She suffered from low self-esteem and did not think she could do any better. But now she said she really did love her husband and wanted to work on improving their life together. They had had many good times together in the past, she said, and she believed that he still loved her. Yes, she realized that he, wittingly or not, had opted for a lifestyle that rendered him incapable of participating in a meaningful love-bond, but she wanted to nurse-maid him back to health. Having made this decision, it would be very *important not to resent the task she had taken on.* This is a general principle that is important for anyone who decides to knowingly stay in an impaired relationship. Resenting her task would mean that she had not really accepted it, that perhaps she was continuing in her relationship with the magical belief that her husband was not really the person he was, that he would just stop drinking himself into oblivion and start caring for her. Another major concern remained—did she continue to think, even subconsciously, that this was the kind of relationship she deserved? She agreed that if this relationship didn't work out, she wouldn't jump into another but would first establish her own independence and then go to the next relationship, not looking for someone to take care of but for someone with whom to share her life. In fact, she was beginning to feel that she was growing beyond her husband, but she loved him and wanted to help him catch up.

Then, at her fourth therapy session, a new problem emerged. She said that her husband had beaten her up. It was a first, but he had said he would do it again if he "had to." She had gotten drunk and passed out in the apartment building swimming pool, nearly drowning herself. If the maintenance man hadn't come along, she would have drowned. It infuriated Scott to see her imitating *his* behavior. If she did it again, he'd give her the beating of her life.

"I guess I deserved it," she said.

"Wait a minute," said her therapist. "You don't really believe that?"

She was silent.

The therapist said, "This is very important. If you don't handle this right, this is how it begins. I mean, a new pattern is established. It will become okay if he beats you."

"But wasn't I asking for it by getting drunk like that? I almost killed myself!"

"I don't disagree that what you did was irresponsible. You're probably feeling guilty about it. That guilt is a psychological symptom that lets you know you violated your own value system. But don't wallow in guilt. That's just as irresponsible. And listen, nothing justifies your husband setting limits on you by beating you up. He's going to do it again unless you make it very clear to him that you absolutely will not tolerate physical violence. He can talk to you, even shout at you, but he cannot hit, slap, kick, or do violence to you in any way."

"Well, he did slap me again this morning, just to remind me, he said. What do I do?"

"Get very clear with him. Let him know that if he lays a hand on you again, no matter what, you will call the police, and he will have to go. Can you do that? Would telling him that be risking getting beaten up? If so, then maybe you should call the police now."

"No, no. I can tell him that."

Later in the session the underlying motive for her own drunken episode revealed itself: "I was so afraid of losing him. I didn't want to be alone. I thought that if I brought myself down to his level, I wouldn't be too good for him." Having clarified this point for herself, she also saw that the consequence of such a strategy would be that she would become as incapable of loving as her husband was incapable of loving her. She determined not to allow violence to become a part of the pattern of their relationship together. "I saw enough of that in the way my father treated my mother," she said. She also decided that an alcoholic husband would not be enough for her indefinitely. He'd have to demonstrate an ability to change his alcohol-based lifestyle, or she'd leave him. When, remains *her decision*.

WHEN IS A LOVER TOO IMPAIRED? (WHEN SHOULD YOU GIVE UP AND FIND ANOTHER FISH IN THE SEA, ONE THAT CAN SWIM?)

First, let us suppose that, using the criteria we've already discussed, you decide that you are in a relationship with an impaired lover. Then if, after honestly considering the evidence, you decide that you yourself are not impaired, you *might* decide to stay in a relationship with an impaired lover. I would suggest that you consider the question, Are you somehow finding happiness even in your relationship with an impaired lover?

Let us look at another example, this time from the popular "soap" *The Young and the Restless*. George Rawlins and Cassandra Hall very much love each other. George, however, has had an accident that has left him impotent. George insists that Cassandra find other lovers, but she insists she loves him alone and that their happiness together is enough for her. They are married. For a time the relationship works, but Cassandra is attracted (as the soap would have it) to George's best friend. The sexual side of her nature presses for expression. Under normal circumstances, she could find fulfillment with George, but he is impaired. Does she remain miserable and frustrated for life? Does she "act out" and experience guilt? Cassandra would be more loving of George and of herself by honestly telling George that their relationship is no longer working for her. To resist the expression of her own sexual nature could, for her, be a kind of psychological self-mutilation (the inflicting on herself of the psychological equivalent of the injury inflicted upon George by accident). The fact that she is no longer happy means that their impaired, temporarily sufficient relationship is no longer sufficient; it has become *too impaired,* and now it is time to move on. Unfortunately, demonstrating a weakness common not just to those in soaps, she does not confront the issue. She has a clandestine affair with George's best friend, experiencing the chronic guilt and insecurity of the betrayer and arousing the all-too-human suspicion of betrayal in the man she once loved. We can only hope that in future episodes she will act on her love for George (and for herself) and tell him what is going on. (You can find an extended treatment of the dilemma of the physically impaired lover in Ernest Hemingway's novel *The Sun Also Rises,* or check out the videotape movie version by the same name.)

The love in romance has to be given out of a commitment to the love-bond, not out of a sense of guilt. If any love-bond is going to work, it cannot be abandoned whenever it is challenged by misfortune—very little love would be involved in such a bond. However, the limits of misfortune that can be tolerated have to be determined by those involved. This is especially true when the misfortune involves the impairment of the capacity to love in one of the partners to a love-bond. If significant impairment involves both partners, then no love-bond exists, regardless of what those involved may think they want.

Disease and accident may be visited upon people that will test the strength of the love-bond to its limit. A competent sailor can easily handle calm seas. Mild storms require more skill. As storms increase in intensity, so does the need for skill, *and* there are storms that nearly no one, no love-bond, can survive. We might question the wisdom, if not the mental health, of those who knowingly put out to sea amid violent storms. But many are caught unaware and find themselves in the midst of a storm without having made the choice to be there. Questions to ask: Will the storm ever end? Is there any happiness and fulfillment in your life? Is happiness your goal? After honestly reflecting upon these questions, you decide when, if ever, to head back to shore and perhaps start out anew with someone else into less stormy seas.

IMPAIRED RELATIONSHIPS BETWEEN IMPAIRED LOVERS

Some relationships are impaired not because either of the lovers is impaired but because basic beliefs and life goals are incompatible.

Can a fundamentalist Christian and an agnostic scientist find happiness in a love-bond with each other?

Can a scientist with a high regard for the reasoning ability of his beloved who discovers that his beloved is a devout believer in astrology or witchcraft continue to live with and love her?

Can an authoritarian love a libertarian and vice versa?

Is a relationship between Edith and Archie Bunker really possible? (Then again would Archie Bunker really be better off with someone just like himself?)

A clash of beliefs within a love-bond can lead to a lot of extra work and, if mutual respect is not maintained, to an impossibly impaired relationship. If, however, lovers knowingly accept the extra work and maintain mutual respect, the loving in such a relationship could result in a mind-expanding experience.

The same can be said for a clash of lifestyles. If you really don't want to be married to an actress or a concert pianist and you determine—after honest discussion and reflection—that acting or concert piano playing is necessary to your lover's happiness, then you should part friends, sad perhaps, but still caring about, not resenting each other. However, I strongly suggest that you at least consider the potential rewards of trying to synthesize a new lifestyle out of your conflicting lifestyles.

Differences between you and your lover in beliefs and lifestyle can, if based on a solid foundation of genuine love, lead to a very strong love-bond. Study, for example, the love-bond in the novel (or movie) *Out of Africa*. Note the depth of love that results between Denys Finch-Hatton and Karen Blixen, despite their very different views of what a relationship is all about.

LOVING THE STRANGENESS AND MYSTERY IN YOUR LOVER

You ought not see impairments where there are none. Remain open to your lover's potential. Two swallows do not a summer make, nor does *strange* mean "crazy." If a camera were to follow anyone through the day, in both public and private moments, and especially if that camera also had the capacity to record thoughts as well as actions and sound, a great deal of what is considered strange would be recorded—*or* the tape would be very boring. A certain strangeness or, more romantically put, mystery, is a trait of anyone who continues to grow intellectually and emotionally. A psychologically healthy person adapts himself to his environment but is not constricted by it. He continues to ask questions, learn new things, develop new talents, and try alternative ways of interacting with the people around him.

Creative geniuses, admired after the fact, were often thought strange during their lifetime. This is not because of any supposed connection between genius and insanity but because in order to make genius-level, creative insights, one must be willing to look at life in different (strange) ways. This is also necesary, not just for geniuses, but for anyone wanting to tap his or her own potential. Part of loving someone is not only tolerating strangeness or mystery within the one we love, but encouraging it.

Each of us, in our attempts to learn, to grow, and to experience life, may—in fact at times must—be unique and creative, and, therefore, seem a little strange. Sad to say, life shuts down prematurely for many. Too often people accept monotonous, unvarying ways of thinking.

The successful romantic love-bond encourages an explosive growth in awareness of self and of the surrounding world, because it requires that the particpants love themselves and each other.

In D. H. Lawrence's novel *The Rainbow*, a husband, used to working the land but not used to thinking, passes through life one day after the other, all days alike, except the numbers on the calendar change. One day he walks into his bedroom to find his pregnant wife dancing in the nude—there always was something peculiar about her that disturbed the monotony of his life.

Not knowing what to make of Anna's behavior, he focuses on the practical issue—she might catch a cold. He is annoyed, though, because he senses in his own way that there is more going on here than meets the eye.

Her behavior is a challenge. It startles him out of his benumbed existence. Rather than accepting the challenge to grow, he resents the disturbance. Life would be more comfortable, it seems, if she would just let things be.

> And she lifted her hands and danced again, to annul him, the light glanced on her knees as she made her slow, fine movements down the far side of the room, across the firelight. He stood away near the door in blackness of shadow, watching transfixed. And with slow, heavy movements she swayed backwards and forwards, like a full ear of corn, pale in the dusky afternoon, threading before the firelight, dancing his non-existence, dancing herself to the Lord, to exultation.
>
> He watched, and his soul burned in him. He turned aside, he could not look, it hurt his eyes. (Viking Compass Edition, pages 180–81.)

An insensitive psychiatrist might be tempted to use the criteria of his trade to suggest that the poor woman is suffering from an "atypical psychosis" of pregnancy, but the label, even if accurate, would be overly simplistic. Her love-bond, though it may be sanctioned by state and church, rather than an occasion for growth, constricts her, just as the straps that used to bind up the feet of Chinese maidens prevented the growth of their feet so that their feet remained forever dainty, though crippled—it was a cultural tradition.

She resented her husband. His constricted view of life constricted her life. She had outgrown him, and he would not grow with her. If she had had more self-confidence, or if the society in which she lived were not so controlling, she would have left him physically. Within her mind she had left him.

By the time the dance scene occurs, their love-bond has deteriorated into a tug-of-war of personalities. Instead of mutual personal growth stimulated by love there is conflict. Neither of them desires the empathy experienced by Karen and Mike in *Brainstorm*. He, threatened by that which he does not understand, resents her and wants to tug her back to the bland normality that he does understand. He can't blame her for her craziness, but nevertheless he senses his own deep deficiency. He has allowed himself to become boring. That is a painful fact about himself that, without her, he would have ignored. She, rather than loving him to this self-awareness, seeks to destroy him with it. He cannot fail to notice the hostility of her dance "to annul him." She makes it impossible for him to accept his new insight. It is as if a thirsty man were being drowned. She is too caught up in her own need and so cannot love him. He is too caught up in the discomfort of confrontation to love her. His response is to turn away from the discomfort: "After this day, the door seemed to be shut on his mind."

Neither bothers to understand the other's need, and the effect is as if they hated each other. Failed love-bonds often end in hate. Along with mutual interests, physical attraction, and so on, love-bonds are built on complementary differences, differences that can be an occasion for growth. Without the commitment to love, once the free ride of falling in love is over, differences may become points of contention and impair communication. Differences may be seen as deficiencies, and knowledge is used to hurt rather than to love.

It is ironic that the very basis of a love-bond can become the basis of hate, but then romantic relationships never turn out right for people who have not learned to love.

Now that he has closed his mind, even the tug-of-war will stop. She may belittle him. If he is prone to violence, he may strike out at her from time to time. Their conflicts are like the spasmodic twitchings of a comatose body. Even if they continue to live together, their home has become a tomb for a dead relationship. If they separate to find other lovers, they will still need to learn to love.

Too often we are weekend lovers, amateurs, approaching love the way we approach weekend tennis, and if tiredness, irritation, or fear enters the picture, it is easy to forget love, as if it weren't important to love consistently despite adversity, as if love can be neglected and then returned to without harm. Would-be lovers ought to remind themselves of Shakespeare's 116th sonnet:

Let me not to the marriage of true minds
Admit impediments. Love is not love
Which alters when it alteration finds,
Or bends with the remover to remove:
O, no! it is an ever-fixed mark,
That looks on tempests and is never shaken;
It is the star to every wandering bark,
Whose worth's unknown, although his height be taken.
Love's not Time's fool, though rosy lips and cheeks
Within his bending sickle's compass come;
Love alters not with his brief hours and weeks,
But bears it out even to the edge of doom.
If this be error, and upon me prov'd,
I never writ, nor no man ever lov'd.

Relationships can be a powerful means of exploring the mystery of life. In the movie *My Dinner with André,* André says to his friend,

> Of course there's a problem, because the closer you come, I think, to another human being, the more completely mysterious and unreachable that person becomes. I mean, you have to reach out. . . .
>
> Have an affair and up to a certain point you can really feel that you are on firm ground. You know, the sexual conquest to be made. There are different questions. Does she enjoy the ears nibbled? How intensely can you talk about Schopenhauer, (or) some elegant French restaurant? Whatever nonsense it is. It's all, I think, to give you the semblance that there's firm earth. Well, have a real relationship with a person that goes on for years. That's completely unpredictable. Then you've cut off all your ties to the land and you're sailing into the unknown, into the uncharted seas.

Relationships that sail into uncharted seas are unusual to the point of strange, but they are not impaired.

Lovers learn genuinely to appreciate the differences in one another and help their relationship grow in a unique way. This is true of any love-bond based on love, and that is what makes each relationship unique.

Chapter 11

LOVERS' REUNION AS MUTUAL VICTORY

You're back with your lover. You may think you've won. But be careful. If you won, did somebody lose? Did you beat out the competition? No. You loved your lover back to you. Did you show your lover that he was wrong for leaving you? No. He probably wasn't wrong, and wrong isn't the point anyway. By loving your lover back to you, you have demonstrated that a love-bond between you and your lover—now and into the future—can be a mutually happy way to live. You certainly have not demonstrated that you were right and somebody else was wrong. The only victory possible in a love-bond is mutual victory, the you-win/I-win kind. Be happy with your reunion and continue to love.

It is when your lover returns to you that you will be the most severely tested. Loving 100 percent may feel less crucial. You may feel that since you worked really hard to get your lover back, now he can do more of the work. To think this is to already be falling back into old patterns that kept your love from working in the first place.

Does a good artist, once he becomes good, exert only a

50 percent effort? Not if he loves his art. He does his 100 percent best with every painting, every sculpture he creates. In the same way the art of loving may come more naturally as you get better at it, but you can never stop loving 100 percent. Remaining aware of the danger of falling back into old patterns that once seemed more natural than loving is vital to the success of your relationship.

SHOULD YOU SHOW THIS BOOK TO YOUR LOVER?

What happens if after you get your lover back, you show him this book? He might glance at it and chuckle and then go about his business. Or he might take the book more seriously, pick it up, look at it intently, and then resent it. "What the hell is this!?" The apparent manipulativeness of your using a strategy to get your lover back can be disconcerting.

By now you've seen that the only thing I advocate manipulating is your own neediness—manipulating it out of the way of your love. Nonetheless, I do suggest that you *not* show this book as part of a strategy of getting your lover back. An artist demonstrates his ability through his art, not by putting the books of technique he has studied on display. You do not, by your action, want to risk apppearing to say, "See how hard I'm working to get you back? The least you could do is come back!" That would be a manipulation-with-guilt maneuver, one of the common mistakes discussed in chapter 3. Nor do you want to issue a challenge: "See, I'm going to get you back regardless of what you think you want to do!" That would be the bravado of the foolish, enraging with its arrogance and convincing only as a demonstration of insecurity, to say nothing of contradicting in action the theoretical strategy you'd be bragging about.

Now, if your lover happens to see this book, you could with a gentle smile and a matter-of-fact or tongue-in-cheek tone, say, "No harm in trying." If your lover wants to discuss the book, nothing wrong with that. If your lover gets angry and argumentative, you've learned in chapter 9 how to deal with that.

Once you get your lover back, then you might share this book with him. A discussion of the ideas contained in it will help prevent your love-bond from being taken for granted and will enhance communication.

When I first told my lover that I was planning to write *How to Get Your Lover Back,* she laughed. So did I. I was serious, but somehow, perhaps because I had so recently "won" her back, the idea seemed funny. When she saw that I was actually writing it, she read the work in progress.

She said, "That's right. Lots of people want to get their lovers back. Just listen to the songs on the radio. They just don't know how to do it."

THE RISK OF FORGETTING TO LOVE 100 PERCENT

Just as individuals have patterns of behavior that are hard to change, so do relationships. Once the pressure is off and the longing in your heart has been replaced by the fulfillment of your lover's return, it is an easy thing to allow your relationship to slip back to what it was.

If your lover finds herself back in the same kind of stale relationship that she once left, the one that wasn't working—she *will* feel tricked, and that's because she will have been tricked. All the loving you demonstrated then becomes a lie. If she leaves again, it will be harder to get her back the next time. Even if she stays, there will be no love-bond, there will be only the dull monotony and chronic resentment of shared stagnation.

When Matt thought he had his lover back, he bragged about his "tactics" to Inge. "I knew when I told you that I loved you and wanted you to stay with me, but that you should go with Zeke if that's what it took to sort out your feelings, I *knew* that would get you." His bragging tone implied trickery, not loving. Inge laughed good-naturedly. She found his comments amusing, but though she had come back to him, her feelings were still a bit confused. She resented his gloating in his apparent power over her. A lovers' reunion is always tentative, tentative because how long a reunion lasts depends on what happens next.

How will Matt respond when he discovers that Inge has not yet let go of her relationship with Zeke? Will he continue to love her 100 percent, or will smugness at thinking himself the victor lead him to slip into old patterns of insensitivity?

Matt thought he had Inge back. He clarified nothing. He just assumed that once she had said yes, then she was back. He had won. The pressure was off. He would not have said so even to himself, but he felt he didn't have to love her so persistently. He was ecstatic. Once again he held her in his arms, and the embrace was mutual.

One night, a mere five days later, Inge came home late in the evening. Matt opened the door and said a confident, "Hello, sweetie."

She glanced at him blankly, walked mutely into the living room. She sat on the floor in front of the stereo. She slipped *The Music of Cosmos* into the cassette deck. (She and Matt had watched every episode of the television series *Cosmos* together. "It's the only thing we ever do together," she had said. "But you like it," he had said. "Yes." Wrapped

up in a blanket together, they had sat in front of the TV.
. . . Now, over a year later, she listened to the music,
oblivious of his presence.) The little door to the cassette
deck clicked shut. She turned the volume down low. Softly
the strains of Vangelis's "Heaven and Hell," time and
distance distilled into music, arrived in the room.

Matt sat back in a low chair. He avoided staring at her
by looking down at the carpet near where she lay. He had
the same feeling he had had when late one night as a little
boy he sat up with his silent, brooding family in the living
room by his grandfather's coffin. Only this time he wasn't
sure what was in the coffin. Her relationship with Zeke?
Or Matt's relationship with her? When he glanced at her,
he noticed that tears ran silently down her cheeks.

"Is there something wrong?" he asked. His words hung
inanely in the soft silence of the music.

She looked up at him, her crying made more apparent
by her tear-moistened eyelashes. "You don't care, do you?"
she asked in a tone of melancholic accusation.

"What do you mean?" he asked, calmly answering her
question with his own. "Don't care about you?" He sus-
pected his question was off the mark.

She stared at him, expressionless, except for the melancholic curiosity in her eyes, studying him as though there
might be explanations inscribed on his face, but certainly
not contained in his words.

He tensed almost imperceptibly, then asked, "It has to
do with Zeke, doesn't it?"

"You don't care. It doesn't matter to you that somebody
else gets hurt, so long as you get me back."

"I didn't ask you to go with him," he said softly. (His
remark is a verbal chess move of the I-win/you-lose type.
Now that he think. he's got her back, he's shifted the
blame of the breakup onto her.)

"It's all your fault," she said. "I didn't know you still

loved me. You didn't show it. If you don't show your love by what you do, is there any love? And what are you doing now? Saying it's all my fault?"

"But you still loved me or were confused enough not to know what your feelings were. You moved in with Zeke prematurely. I don't mean to pass judgment, but don't you think that if a relationship were to break up, it's important to have a period by yourself before getting involved with someone else?" (He says he doesn't mean to, but he is passing judgment. He is struggling with her to win an argument. His words indicate that he now gives placing blame a high priority.)

"I was by myself for a long time," she said softly, acidly. "We may have been living together, but I was by myself." (She's answered his verbal chess game with an effective countermove.)

"I'm sorry if Zeke has to get hurt, but . . ." (He's retreated from their argument without acknowledging the accuracy of her observtion, and now he's trying to reassure himself that he's still the victor by expressing sorrow for the defeated "competition.")

"No, you're not sorry. You don't care about anybody's feelings but your own. You just want me to come back to you just like that." She clicked her fingers. "Who cares whose feelings get hurt?"

"I love you, and I believe you love me. If that means Zeke gets hurt, I'm sorry, but that's the way it is. If it had gone the other way, I'd be licking my wounds. But damn it," he added, echoing the melodramatic words of *Wuthering Heights*, "you love me. How dare you sacrifice that love to appease your guilt?" He regretted his words immediately. She hadn't actually sacrificed her love, yet. (He is being insensitive to Inge's feelings and claiming to love her at the same time.)

"Listen to you!" she declared. "Matt knows everything.

He knows my feelings better than I do. Well, I'm not so sure anymore, Matt. I'm not so sure."

"Not sure about what?"

"I don't know who I love. You gloat over your, quote, 'victory,' unquote. You even said the best move you made was when you said I should go to Colorado with Zeke if that's what I needed, you'd wait for me. Quote, 'a brilliant move,' unquote. You just knew that would get me back, didn't you? It's all a game to you, and I'm a pawn in a chess game or a puppet on strings."

I knew it was a mistake to gloat. I had to be a goddamn braggart, he thought to himself. "Look, I'm sorry, but I *was* sincere about what I said. I still am." He felt his heart rate pick up and a queasy emptiness overcome him. He was glad he was sitting down. "I still say that if you need to go to Colorado to resolve your feelings, then that's what you ought to do, but if you feel you have to see Zeke when you get back, I won't be able to see you. I can't spend time with you if you're still seeing him." (Matt is trying to manipulate Inge through a take-away he doesn't really believe in.)

"I'm not sure about anything anymore," she said ambiguously.

"It's not resolved, then." The energy in his voice waned.

Her eyes closed gently, sadly. She lay in a semifetal position on the carpet. He watched her breathing until tiredness overcame him, then he got a blanket and a pillow. He covered her with the blanket and tucked the pillow beneath her head.

He asked, "Honey, do you want to sleep here or in bed?"

"Here," she said.

"Okay," he said firmly, resignedly, a little angrily.

He reached for the stereo deck.

Her words interrupted his gesture, "Let it play, please." She asked, her eyes remaining closed, as if she talked in her sleep, "Are you angry with me?"

"I'm angry and I'm not angry. Let's talk tomorrow."
No response. She was already sleeping.

After getting his lover back, Matt regressed to his old less-than-100-percent loving style. For starters, he attempted to blame Inge for seeking out Zeke in the first place. This contradicted the approach he used to get her back and injured his credibility. If establishing a successful love-bond is the goal, then the question of blame is trivial, unimportant, an utter waste of energy, even if his partner blamed him—which in this case she did primarily in response to his remark, "I didn't ask you to go with him."

Then he attempted to force her back to him by threatening a manipulative take-away. If Matt were to be sensitive and understanding—the way he was when he was loving her 100 percent—he could help her sort out her feelings or allow her the space she needs to sort them out. If he doesn't establish the pattern of understanding rather than blaming, there will be trouble in the future, even if Zeke disappears from the picture, because the habit of blaming will have established itself, and it is likely to become mutual. Now, in addition to her unresolved feelings about Zeke—whatever they are—she's got the added confusion of Matt's sudden insensitivity.

Inge's sudden confusion as she shifted away from someone else and back to Matt provided another opportunity for Matt to demonstrate the strength of his love. If in the future Inge were to make a habit of jumping back to Zeke from time to time (and there is no reason to believe she would), Matt could then focus more and more of his energy on the other aspects of his life, always remaining positive and loving when he is with Inge but *not* immediately dropping whatever he is doing and running back to her—this is the fine art of the Loving Take-Away. This is how he could, if he needed to, negotiate the tricky balance of being understanding and setting limits.

Matt had been startled by the sudden discovery that his apparent success was not as certain as he thought it was. He set himself up for this unpleasant discovery by his smugness. Now he was determined to make up for his mistake, but Inge had left Honolulu that morning and was not due back for two weeks. What happened next?

Matt spent the next afternoon correcting an essay test he had given his students. After the first time through, he realized he had been too harsh on his students. So he started recorrecting the tests. He felt he had failed his own first test of loving Inge once he got her back. He didn't want to punish others for his own emotional turmoil; he wanted another chance with Inge. Halfway through the second attempt at correcting, he admitted to himself that his concentration was off. He'd have to correct the essay test a third time. Then the phone rang. He had already answered the phone half a dozen times that day, thinking each time that it might be Inge.

"Hello."

"Hi, Matt," said Inge tentatively.

"Inge! Hello," he said with obvious relief. "It's good to hear your voice."

"I thought you were angry with me," matter-of-factly, no longer tentative.

"I think I was, but I'm still happy to hear your voice."

"And I was angry with you. So I guess we were both angry."

"Well, how are you now?" he asked.

"I don't know. I was wondering how *we* are. Things weren't going well when I left. I had thought we might talk at the airport, but when you asked me in the car about Zeke, you seemed so smug, as if you knew how things would turn out and you were enjoying your power."

"Actually I was scared. Sometimes I act smug when I'm scared."

"Scared?"

"Well, nervous. I let the fear of losing you get the upper hand. I was starting to see our relationship like some kind of contest with Zeke, and I felt I was being cheated out of winning, but that was wrong. I was wrong. Look, I love you. I really, really love you. It just doesn't make any sense for me to try to force you back to me. I just assumed you would get rid of . . . take care of whatever was keeping us apart. Only by making assumptions like that, *I'm* keeping us apart. I'm here for you if you want me. If you've got to sort something out, if I can help, I will . . . or I'll wait. And you don't have to feel like my waiting for you is a burden. My saying this is not a game, Inge, believe me. It's reality, because to do it any other way would not be loving you. I'll be okay whatever happens. It's just that I'd rather be okay with you than without you."

She answered, "Emotions can be confusing sometimes, for both of us."

"Can I help?"

"No, I'll sort things out. I'm sorry if I've confused you."

"That's okay. I've done my share of confusing things."

"Matt, you know you've got me back."

"Now that you've just said it again, I do."

"Well, I meant it when I said it the first time. Do I still have *you* back?" she asked.

"Yes, of course," he said with a happy laugh. Then he asked, "There's something else?"

"It's just that I was upset, because our whole breakup seemed unnecessary. Why did this confusion have to happen in the first place? Why couldn't you have just been there? I would never have left you, but I never really felt the comfort of us being together. Even when you were there, there was always something missing. Every time I started to feel comfortable with you, you were suddenly distant. The feeling I'd get was as if I went to lay my head down on a pillow, the best, most comfortable pillow in the world, only to discover there was no pillow, maybe no bed, just an empty room with a bare floor. That's the way our relationship felt."

"I'm sorry, Inge. At the time of our breakup, and before it, I didn't understand what I was doing. I'm better at handling relationships now. I don't have a time machine to go back and do it better then, but I can do it better now. And I will keep on doing it better, if I get the chance."

"*We've* got the chance," she said.

"That's great!" he said.

A long pause, then she said, "What time is it there?"

"Oh . . . ah," he looked at his watch, a little surprised to consider such a practical question at a time like this. "It's five o'clock."

"It's nine P.M. here, and there's a beautiful full moon. The night is softly glowing, Matt."

He laughed in relief at the warmth of her remark. "I can just imagine. I can hardly wait until it's nine P.M. here as well."

Two weeks later, when she returned to Honolulu, she told him, "It's strange. It's like there's you and there's me, and then there's a whole new thing—you *and* me."

She handed him a note that he had given her months ago, shortly after she had first left him. He had told her at that time that if she ever wanted "to redeem" the note, she need only hand it to him.

The note read:

1. Be with me.
2. Go on trip to Colorado with me.
3. Marry me.
4. ———. (Blank space, indicating "whatever.")

He smiled sheepishly. "All four?"

God (or the Cosmos) help him if he didn't really mean it.

ALTERNATIVE ENDINGS

There is more than one possible ending to the story of Matt and Inge. Perhaps Matt goes on loving, and Inge cannot help but continue to love him in return. Even after he gets her back, he never allows himself to take her or his relationship with her for granted. He reminds himself that it is wrong to assume that it is possible to know all there is to know about a lover, that lovers by definition continue to grow and make new discoveries about themselves and each other. It is not the same old song played over and over again, which, no matter how enjoyable the first time around, becomes too predictable and no longer excites the old enthusiasm. It's a song with endless variation, proof that happiness can go on forever.

Or perhaps Matt slips into his old ways. Inge once again begins to feel unloved. The bickering begins. There are arguments that seem to have no point, because the point lies deeper than words.

On warm nights he walks outside their house, looks up at the stars, wonders what it would be like to vacation in Europe alone, to go to Venice, say, and sitting at a small table in St. Mark's Square, drink cappuccino and strike up conversations with Italian girls. The bands at the outdoor cafés provide a musical backdrop, to say nothing of the Renaissance architecture and the canals. What if he got there, all that distance from Inge, and the old longing returned to his soul? Life has many possibilities. To choose one sometimes means to lose another. One cannot walk in two directions at once. The choice is one of lifestyle—

diversity versus deeply plumbing one true love. Matt imagines himself in Venice. He finds himself thinking the words *I love you, Inge. I wish you were here.*

SOME SPECULATIONS ON THE NATURE OF RELATIONSHIPS

Real commitment is not possible unless you are aware that you have made a choice. Too often social, cultural, and familial forces pressure people into lifestyles they would not have chosen for themselves and with which they are not compatible. To use an old metaphor, not everyone is made from the same mold. The fact that other molds exist need not be a threat to the contour of *your* life—the existence of other kinds of life means you have more than one option. If you let another person or persons make that choice for you, you could become incredibly unhappy, wonder if your nonchoice was the right thing for you, and out of fear of making a choice and deeply buried doubts about the way your life is going, you might even ridicule other lifestyles. If you are genuinely happy and your life is working for you, other people will take note, and by your example they will know your way.

Sexual orientation is fundamental to personality structure. A homosexual does no one any favors if he forces himself into a heterosexual love-bond. To do so is a violation of his own integrity, and inconsiderate of his partner. If he's bisexual, he could—if he really wants to—make the choice of a heterosexual love-bond, thereby leaving undeveloped the homosexual aspect of his personality. Homosexuals do have meaningful heterosexual relationships in which the purpose is to have children with a partner who is informed of the limitations of the relationship—a platonic love-bond, and deep, meaningful friendship can be formed. Honesty, as in all relationships, is essential.

Beyond the basic sexual orientation of a person, there are a whole range of lifestyles; the long-term, deeply committed, monogamous love-bond that has been the focus of this book is just one kind. There is the single's lifestyle in which basically you go it on your own, enjoying the company of other people but not getting involved in romance, although sex between friends remains a healthy possibility. (See *Sex Without Love* by Russell Vannoy.) There is also polygamy, married or otherwise. Many people, as evidenced by their behavior, seem to be naturally polygamous. In the dominant culture the polygamous lifestyle may violate a lot of assumed traditions but there would be a lot more honesty, and a lot less suffering, if the people who do would just admit that they prefer polygamy, at least part of the time, and sometimes all of the time. Honesty and love are possible outside of the traditional long-term love-bond. Probably the lifestyle most people settle into is most accurately described as "serial monogamy," which may or may not be interspersed with periods of polygamy.

Remember, if genuine loving rather than controlling is what is important to you, then people have a choice as to how to pursue happiness, and one should respect, even if one does not advocate, the choices that other people make. Only in the context of a recognition of options and a respect for choice does the long-term monogamous love-bond have value. If you ignore choice, you choose hypocrisy. To put it another way, you cannot escape freedom.

Chapter 12
SUMMARY AND
YOUR PRESCRIPTIONS

In his book *The Art of Loving* Erich Fromm writes, "The difficulty of the problem [of learning how to practice the art of loving] is enhanced by the fact that most people today, hence many readers of this book, expect to be given prescriptions of 'how to do it yourself.' " Yet his publishers have advertised his work with the following claim: "The World-Famous Psychoanalyst's Daring Prescription For Love." Aside from his publisher's understandable desire to "hype" his book, the problem at the root of this apparent conflict of opinion may lie in what exactly is meant by *prescription*. People desiring a simple fix, such as a pill or advice about what to do in a particular instance, are likely to be disappointed, unless (a) they *take* the pill, bearing in mind possible risks versus benefits; and (b) they learn to grasp the principle behind the advice about a particular instance so that they can adjust their actions to changing circumstances.

I have given many examples with variation in circumstance so that you can understand how to apply the principles of this book, just as in watching a tennis game you learn to apply the principles, though the exact circumstances of the game vary endlessly. The prescription that provides a guide or principle for action can be very useful, but remember to modify the dosage to fit *your* specific illness.

Bad prescriptions of what to do about failed romantic love litter conversations on the subject:

"It just wasn't meant to be."

A love-bond cannot last unless you mean for it to last. It doesn't just happen, nor does it just fade away.

"The chemistry is either there or it isn't."

If a love-bond existed, then the chemistry was there, and how you treat each other can elicit or destroy hidden chemistry.

"You can't force someone to love you, so give up."

It is true that you can't *force* someone to love you. To even attempt to do so means that you do not love the someone you're trying to force. You *can* dramatically increase the likelihood of someone loving you by genuinely loving him or her.

"You can't solve relationships the way you solve equations."

Relationships can be "solved," if by solving one means understanding.

THE SUMMARY (OR THE LONG FORM OF THE PRESCRIPTIONS)

1. Before you do anything else, relax, so that you can calmly plan your course of action. Keep thinking the word *relax* until your mind remembers the meaning of the word. It is important to gain understanding of what is happening in your love life, if possible, *before* your next contact with your lover. Understanding occurs best in a state of alert relaxation.

2. Ask yourself honestly, "Do I really want to get my lover back?" If there has been genuine love in your relationship, and if you still love your ex-lover, then you may benefit both of you by getting your lover back. In fact, not getting your lover back may mean that the two of you have lost an opportunity to learn how to make a love-bond work. There are many fish in the sea, but you may get to know quite a few of them without ever having learned how to love any of them.

3. If you have decided that you want your lover back, be honest with yourself about the reason. A bruised ego and the need to be wanted by a significant other should not be misconstrued as love. Do you want your lover back so that you can drop your lover rather than be dropped? Is it to allow yourself more time to adjust to an inevitable breakup? Or is it because you want to re-create a love-bond? Any of these may be sufficient reason for getting a lover back, but it will help you to gauge the amount of effort you wish to make and to hold your own hurt in perspective if you understand the "why" behind your actions.

4. Inventory your needs, so that they don't take you by surprise.

5. Remind yourself repeatedly that your needs take second place to salvaging your relationship.

6. Love and honor yourself. Without self-love you are standing in quicksand, no matter what kind of relationship you are in.

7. Do not neglect work interests, friends, hobbies, or physical exercise—these are signs of self-love and make you more lovable. When thoughts about your ex-lover intrude at inappropriate times, think, "Later." There should be scheduled times when you allow yourself to think about your ex-lover.

8. Make a commitment to yourself to love your lover 100 percent. To love means to demonstrate an active caring for the needs and personal growth of your lover. It also means that you will not tolerate physical or emotional abuse.

9. Recognize and avoid the common mistakes of jealousy. Never insist on sex. Do not make demands and ultimatums. Do not try to evoke pity or guilt and make no direct or indirect threats of any kind.

10. Be honest with yourself about the role of sex in your relationship. Did a problem with sex damage your relationship? Educate yourself about sexual styles, about sexual technique, and about the need—no matter how good the technique—for genuine passion.

11. Use positive visualization: Imagine moments when you and your lover are happy together. The emphasis should not be on the fantasy of the relief of your own need. Do not torture yourself by visualizing your lover with someone else.

12. Ask for time together, but do not demand, beg, or cry for it. It is impossible to demonstrate 100 percent love if time together, necessary as it may be, is obtained by demanding, begging, or crying. If all contact is refused, do not panic or pressure for contact. Periodically make your presence known.

13. Turn all encounters into pleasant encounters (even if the purpose of the encounter is unpleasant). This includes making arrangements to move out, dividing up belongings, dates, chance meetings, doing income tax, going for dental appointments together, or whatever.

14. Use the Ben Franklin Technique to handle disagreements and the Porcupine Technique to handle verbal abuse. Remove yourself from the scene if there is the threat of physical abuse.

15. Once a significant amount of positive time together has been shared (enough to heal over memories of negative times together), use the Loving Take-Away.

• To do so prematurely is a mistake, but as long as you do it gently, without open threat of love withdrawal or the challenge of "either-or," you will enhance your chances of success.

• Not to do so may lead to your being taken for granted, and being taken for granted *will* endanger your chances, prolong your campaign to get your lover back, and, if you get your lover back, will hand over all the power to your lover and undermine the foundation of a healthy love-bond.

16. Do not move in with your lover or allow your lover to move in with you unless all contact with other lovers is broken. Do not demand that contact be broken. If your lover needs time to figure out his or her priorities, then let him do so. You still want to see your lover, even if you are not living together, but ultimately your position should be "I love you one hundred percent, and it has got to be one hundred percent in return."

17. Periodically reread this chapter as a reminder to yourself of the basic approach to use. This will help prevent the natural tendency to slip back into old habits.

18. Once you get your lover back, if you want the love-bond to last, keep on loving. If you've changed your mind, then the loving thing to do would be to let your lover know.

Remember that the long-term, monogamous love-bond is just one of many possible ways in the pursuit of happiness. It is your way only if you choose it to be.

THE PRESCRIPTIONS (EVERYTHING IN THIS BOOK DISTILLED INTO CAPSULE FORM):

Blase Harris, M.D.
Psychiatry

Name REJECTED LOVER   Date WHENEVER

Address WHEREVER

AT ALL TIMES HONOR
AND RESPECT YOURSELF.

Refill ∞   *Blase Harris* M.D.

No Generic Substitute   DEA No._____

Blase Harris, M.D.
Psychiatry

Name REJECTED LOVER   Date WHENEVER

Address WHEREVER

LOVE YOUR EX-LOVER 100%.
(CAUTION: THOUGH THERE IS NO RISK OF OVERDOSE,
THERE IS A RISK OF SERIOUS SIDE EFFECTS, IF
YOU DON'T MAKE VERY CERTAIN THAT YOU KNOW
WHAT "LOVING 100%" MEANS.)

Refill ∞   *Blase Harris* M.D.

No Generic Substitute   DEA No._____

RECOMMENDED
ADDITIONAL READING

For those interested in further study of romantic relationships, the following books are recommended. They are not meant to be all-inclusive, but rather to provide a strong foundation to build upon.

NONFICTION

The Art of Loving, by Erich Fromm (New York: Perennial Library, 1974).

In psychotherapy, or serious discussion, whenever anyone mentions the word *love,* I attempt to determine what he or she means by it. I sometimes suggest the book *The Art of Loving,* a short work, with only a modest amount of psychological jargon, that quickly helps separate love from the emotional dependency and longing with which it is often confused.

Honoring the Self—The Psychology of Confidence and Respect, by Nathaniel Branden (New York: Bantam, 1985).

Whatever your method in the pursuit of happiness, love of and respect for yourself is the necessary first step. This book explores that first step and the effect it can have on the rest of your life, including the effect on the nature of your relationships with others, romantic and otherwise.

Games People Play, by Eric Berne, M.D. (New York: Ballantine, 1985).
This is an excellent introduction to the complex patterns of interaction people develop in their relationships. Do not be put off by the analogy with "games." We all play by unspoken sets of rules in our relationships. The idea is to make sure that the object of the "game" and the purpose of the rules is mutual happiness.

Games Alcoholics Play, by Claude Steiner, Ph.D. (New York: Ballantine, 1984).
This book applies the general principles found in *Games People Play* to an in-depth analysis of the unspoken sets of rules by which alcoholics play. Insights from this book can also be used to better understand relationship "scripts" that involve self-destructive use of other drugs.

What to Say When You Talk to Your Self, by Shad Helmstetter, Ph.D. (New York: Pocket Books, 1987).
One of my patients complained that this book was "poorly written . . . too much of a sales pitch." Nevertheless, even she agreed that the central point of the book was important, and the point is that beginning early in our childhood, people around us put ideas or beliefs into our heads by saying them over and over again. The subconscious will believe anything that is repeated often enough. These ideas and beliefs then become incorporated into our thoughts—often below the surface of awareness—and become life directives. They can be very destructive, or they can be life-enhancing. It is important to uncover your life directives, identify them, and determine if they should be replaced. Dr. Helmstetter describes a useful technique for doing this and gives many examples of positive and negative life directives, some of which you may recognize as being your own.

Love and Addiction, by Stanton Peele with Archie Brodsky (New York: New American Library, 1976).

A careful reading of this book could prevent you from ever confusing love with its counterfeit form, "love addiction," again. Unfortunately Mr. Peele's case examples lack the detail that would make them compelling, and he underestimates the potential power of psychotherapy, as well as of his own book, in assisting people to change their lives. He presents a good analysis of the addiction-bonds and the contrasting love-bond found in D. H. Lawrence's *Women in Love.*

Of Love and Lust, by Theodor Reik (New York: Harcourt Brace Jovanovich, 1976).

I recommend Dr. Reik's book with great caution. He has an unfortunate, but strong tendency to restrict the "natural" lifestyles of men and women into narrow, rigid stereotypes, adopting Sigmund Freud's nineteenth-century Viennese prejudices along with his insights. He writes, for example, "Women are capable of abstract thought, but they don't like it." Nevertheless, *Of Love and Lust* is recommended for its brilliant analysis of the way the mind can transform envy and jealousy into love.

FICTION

Though there is no substitute for the experience of your own life, quality fiction can be a shortcut to useful vicarious experiences in your project to gain increased understanding of human interaction. Quality fiction turns out to be more "real" than the usual brief scenarios that one finds in nonfiction; it more effectively draws you into the experience and exposes you to the subtle detail that the broad overviews of nonfiction usually lack. Perhaps feeling safer behind the veil of fiction, authors reveal more of the truth of human interaction than would otherwise be possible. (I believe that training programs in psychiatry and psychology could be greatly enhanced by the rigorous study of world literature.)

Wuthering Heights, by Emily Brontë (New York: New American Library, 1959).

A dramatic romance that demonstrates the allure of the unhealthy desire to escape oneself by "romanticized" fusion with another. Misunderstood, it has probably contributed to the cultural myth that a passionate romance can make an unhappy person happy. Cathy's description (to Nelly) of her love for Heathcliff reveals the intensity of her need to find the missing part of herself: "My love for Heathcliff resembles the eternal rocks beneath—a source of little visible delight, but necessary. Nelly, I am Heathcliff! He's always, always in my mind—not as a pleasure, any more than I am always a pleasure to myself, but as my own being. So don't talk of our separation again; it is impracticable."

Gone with the Wind, by Margaret Mitchell (New York: Avon Books, 1973).

In the opening scene Scarlett O'Hara demonstrates the fine art of flirtation. Throughout the book, she demonstrates how to manipulate men who confuse their desire for her with love. Rhett Butler demonstrates persistent love (of a lover who is impaired by her own emotional immaturity until the end of the book). And, finally, Scarlett shows how to handle rejection when you want to get your lover back.

A Midsummer Night's Dream, by William Shakespeare (New York: Pocket Books, 1958).

Shows how crazy and humorous love can be when it is confused with falling in love. It is incredible that this play is sometimes categorized as a children's play. Only experienced adults could fully appreciate the subtle as well as the blatant humor and sobering insights of a play that so well depicts romantic love in action, reaction, and crossover action.

The French Lieutenant's Woman, by John Fowles (New York: Little, Brown and Company, 1970).

Charles, an uptight Victorian, begins having his mind and emotional repertoire stretched by a falling-in-love experience with the un-Victorian Sarah, who wears *no hypocrisy, no hysteria, no mask.* The experience is apparently mutual, and the beginnings of a genuine love-bond emerge. However, by the time Charles extracts himself from his inhibitions, he has lost the opportunity.

The double ending is intense romantic drama at its best. In neither ending does he deserve to get his lover back, but in the second, which is not as convincing as the first, Charles "lucks out"—Sarah loves him despite his preoccupation with his own need.

Women in Love, by D. H. Lawrence (New York: Penguin Books, 1976).

In chapter four of this thirty-one-chapter book, Gerald Crich declares, "I don't believe a woman, and nothing but a woman will ever make my life." Ironically he hasn't discovered anything else in life. He grasps at things to fill the emptiness in his soul, including the woman (Gudrun Brangwen) he imagines himself in love with. She and he engage in a passionate struggle of egos. Finally she tires of the struggle and finds entertainment elsewhere. He becomes the enraged, jealous lover—ultimately pathetic and finally a suicide.

In chapter five, Rupert Birkin (a thinly disguised D. H. Lawrence) in a philosophical discussion with Gerald says, "I find . . . that one needs some one really pure single activity—I should call love a single pure activity." He breaks off his relationship with the emotionally sterile Hermione (after she hits him in the head with a stone paperweight) and then develops a genuine love-bond with Ursula Brangwen, Gudrun's sister. He, however, recognizes that the fulfilled life requires more than an isolated love-bond; it requires an enjoyment of life, including friendships. He is saddened by

Gerald's suicide, because Gerald was a potential friend, but Gerald ultimately rejected the friendship.

The Portrait of a Lady, by Henry James (Boston: Houghton Mifflin Company, 1963).

Though Henry James generally distanced himself from the passionate, physical side of romantic love, he was a very keen observer, and paints a subtle portrait of a woman and the multiple suitors who fail to "win" her. The man who does "win" her adroitly maneuvers her into marriage by becoming a challenge because he does not flaunt his desire for her and does not seem to need her. He turns out not to love her, but simply prizes her as a possession.

Rock Island Line, by David Rhodes (New York: Harper & Row, 1975).

Extremely well written and extremely perceptive portrayal of human relationships, including the importance of the passionate, physical side of romantic love. Multiple genuine, unromanticized, first-class love-bonds, especially the relationship between July and Mal, which demonstrates quite clearly how two psychologically intact people are able to accelerate their own and one another's emotional and intellectual growth through love. The most rewarding novel I have read.

Nickel Mountain, by John Gardner (New York: Ballantine, 1975).

Nothing unusual about the story itself, except the care with which the central theme of a love-bond is depicted. Middle-aged, overweight Henry Soames marries Callie, a pregnant sixteen-year-old girl. Their love-bond grows in depth and quality and includes their son and friends—even when they make mistakes, their caring for each other remains constant.

"Vlemk the Box-Painter," a short story, by John Gardner, in *The Art of Living and Other Stories* (New York: Ballantine, 1983).

The story has a fairy-tale quality—the Princess, the artist box-painter, and the portrait of the Princess that's so real that it talks. Beneath the engaging fairy-tale surface, love is in action. Both the Princess and the box-painter bring each other to life, just as the box-painter brought his painting to life. Despite the trappings, the details are realistic.